METHODISM & POLITICS

1791–1851

METHODISM & POLITICS
1791-1851

by

E. R. TAYLOR, B.A.

THIRLWALL AND GLADSTONE
PRIZE ESSAY
1933

CAMBRIDGE
AT THE UNIVERSITY PRESS
1935

CAMBRIDGE
UNIVERSITY PRESS

University Printing House, Cambridge CB2 8BS, United Kingdom

Cambridge University Press is part of the University of Cambridge.

It furthers the University's mission by disseminating knowledge in the pursuit of
education, learning and research at the highest international levels of excellence.

www.cambridge.org
Information on this title: www.cambridge.org/9781316626184

© Cambridge University Press 1935

First published 1935
First paperback edition 2016

A catalogue record for this publication is available from the British Library

ISBN 978-1-316-62618-4 Paperback

To

MY FATHER AND MOTHER
IN AFFECTION AND
GRATITUDE

CONTENTS

PREFACE

Despite the popularity of the study of social and political history, there has been a gap in historical research where the relations between religion and politics have been concerned. What work has already been done in this field has been devoted rather to the social influence exerted by religious forces than to an estimate of the extent to which religion in England has affected the historic party system. Professor Trevelyan has, in his *England under Queen Anne*, recorded the religious division which divided Whigs and Tories in that era of great "party heats", but no one has, as yet, attempted to find reasons for those alliances between Dissenter and Whig, and between Anglican and Tory, which have played so important a part in the history of English politics.

To discover the historical reasons for these alliances was an aim much too ambitious for a Thirlwall Dissertation, but, within the limits of the work, some attempt has been made to look for the factors which influenced the political thought of men in a rapidly changing half-century of English life, and to estimate the relative importance of religious, political, social, and economic forces therein. It was thought best that the investigation should cover the sixty years following the death of John Wesley, because it was in that period that the character of the Church he founded changed. It is a period, both in the life of Methodism and in the life of the nation, in which change was everywhere at work. The length of the period makes it possible to follow out developments to their historical issues, without being either too long to admit of research or too short to have general interest.

The aim and scope of the work is more fully described in Chapter I, but, if this essay discovers reasons for the historical alliances of the two great branches of English Protestantism with the two historic political parties, it will have succeeded in its object. It may be that Methodism, with its connexions with both Church and Dissent, and with its political attachments to both parties, may be the body best fitted to reward such an investigation. In any case, it may be hoped that more work will be done in a field which has so long lain fallow. The interest in the relations between Church and State, which has been quickened by recent events in Germany, might here find profitable expression. If so, we may come to know much of value about the relationship between English religion and the history of party politics in England.

To thank all those who have helped, either by suggestion, criticism, or loan of books or notes, would take too long, but it ought to be mentioned that much of the most valuable assistance I have received has come from those people who prefaced their remarks with the comment: "Of course, I know nothing at all about the subject, but it has always seemed to me that...". To all of them I am most grateful. A word of special thanks is also due to Rev. Dr H. B. Workman for his criticisms, to my friend Rev. C. R. B. Shapland for criticism during the revision, to Miss Ivy K. Johns for preparing the typescript, to Mr K. L. Mowl for preparing the Index, and to the Adjudicators for the Thirlwall Prize and the Syndics of the Cambridge University Press for allowing me thoroughly to revise the Essay.

E. R. T.

December 1934

CHAPTER I

RELIGION AND POLITICS. METHODISM AND THE ENGLISH PARTY SYSTEM

Party strife in English politics has been conditioned by a peculiarly English division—that between the Church and Dissent. It is a division which finds no parallel abroad, but one which has run right across English social and political life. Throughout modern history it has been the dominant factor in determining the political allegiances of Englishmen. Whatever else might vary, that has remained stable. Whilst self-interest and views on home and foreign policy may at various times have inclined men to one side or to the other, whilst party programmes have been completely reversed, and whilst the social classes from which parties have been recruited have been transformed, this opposition of Churchman and Dissenter has remained. Professor Trevelyan[1] finds in its permanence the historical basis of the English party system.

Other countries have copied English institutions and English forms of government, but no country has adopted the true English "two-party system". Because it has

---

[1] The author wishes to express his indebtedness to Professor Trevelyan, not only for his books and lectures, which have supplied much inspiration and guidance, but also for his personal interest and his help some years ago, at the time when the author, whilst still an undergraduate, was first beginning to think about the problem of the connexion between Nonconformity and Liberalism.

sprung up as a product of English social and religious life, it has been impossible to transplant it into countries where its religious foundation would have been exotic. Elsewhere, party alignments have followed social, economic, or personal factions, they have been inspired by class feeling, by abstract political ideas, by economic interests, or by personal loyalties; nowhere but in England have they had as their root cause a religious or ecclesiastical divergence of opinion.

French "Étatisme", which would tolerate no *imperia in imperio*, would never have allowed religious denominations to become the basis for rival political parties. The Revocation of the Edict of Nantes did more than begin the virtual extermination of French Protestantism; it made impossible the religious leadership of a struggle for freedom such as has been in the world of politics the greatest contribution of English Dissent. By reinforcing a tendency towards centralisation, it destroyed hopes of constitutional opposition to the entrenched powers in the name of civil and religious liberty. In the seventeenth century, France sacrificed all to the ideal of strong centralised control over the whole of its political life; in the eighteenth century, through the lack of any constitutional opposition, its government fell before the violence of politically untrained enthusiasts. The subsequent unsettled history of France, with its unstable ministries and its multiple-party system, allied to a strong tradition of centralisation, contrasts sharply with the English system that combines stable government with decentralisation and a tradition of "Freedom". It is not unreasonable to see such a difference of political development as in some measure the fruit of different religious development.

In France, opposition to the central power has had to seek expression in revolution aiming at the overthrow of the governors and their system; in England it has (without disturbing the machinery of government) found a means of criticising and modifying the measures introduced by those with whom it has disagreed. The function of "His Majesty's Opposition" has been to compete with the "Ministerial" party for a share in ruling the kingdom. In the seventeenth and eighteenth centuries Frenchmen were politically educated either to obey or to contemplate resistance to the State;[1] Englishmen were learning to contend against a rival party. In consequence, English political life has been more vigorous and at the same time less violent than French.

The reason is to be found in the religious history of the two nations. Huguenot "Nonconformity" was stamped out in France in the seventeenth century, and all subsequent attempts to supply any Dissenting element were equally unsuccessful. Absolutism demanded complete conformity—in religion as in all else. In England the result of the religious controversy was different. Elizabeth and her Parliament had hoped that the compromise of their Church Settlement would "comprehend" all classes within the Commonwealth; but persecution could not vanquish the militant Puritans who refused to sacri-

[1] Louis XIV's reputed saying "L'État, c'est moi" explains not only the meaning of "State" here, but also the reason for this feature of French political life. Seventeenth-century France equated the "State" and the King. The confusion was to be disastrous in 1789.

fice their conceptions of the truth to the Elizabethan ideal. In the Civil War they were the stalwarts of the Parliamentary side, and, if their triumph was short-lived, they again weathered the storm of persecution under the Restoration monarchy, and won toleration after the English Revolution. Events in France strengthened their position. Exiled Huguenots swelled their numbers, and English sympathy for the victims of an irresponsible Catholic autocrat led to the growth of a toleration which was one of the greatest achievements of the Augustan Age in England. Though still hampered by restrictions and prejudice, they henceforward formed the strength of the Whig party in the country, and by their energy, wealth and influence, gave their support to that party which had traditionally opposed the absolutism of the Crown.

The existence of a recognised Opposition both in politics and religion has left a deep mark upon English history. It has modified the bitterness which has so often characterised political and religious animosities on the Continent; it has, by supplying a vehicle for the expression of grievances and disagreements, made unnecessary those doctrinaire statements of opinion, which inflamed the most violent passions of the French Revolution; it has ministered to the Englishman's love of compromise; and finally, as it has saved England from revolution, it has saved her from atheism.

Where there has only been one form of ecclesiastical organisation, men who have quarrelled with the Church and its representatives have usually withdrawn their allegiance from institutional religion altogether. In England,

4

a man who has found himself at variance, either with his vicar or with the system of the Established Church, has transferred his membership to the "Chapel". English Nonconformity has been more than a positive statement of ecclesiastical ideals; it has been a religious "safety valve". Many a Christian democrat, after a quarrel with an autocratic vicar, has found a more congenial spiritual home in a Dissenting Chapel. He has been saved from the anti-clericalism, which on the Continent has been predominantly atheist; for, in England, anti-clericalism has found its expression in an alternative system of Church government.

This difference in the history of religion has been accompanied by a difference in the character of the opposition to political authority in England and on the Continent. An essential characteristic of Liberalism is the championship of individual liberty against irresponsible authority. The expression of this aim may vary under varying conditions, but it nevertheless remains a *sine qua non* of Liberalism. Democracy, Representative Government, Universal Franchise, Free Trade—all are ideas springing from this essential individualism. Where the Church has been part of the established system, Liberalism has often found itself in opposition to the Church. In countries where there has been no positive ecclesiastical alternative, Liberalism has usually become negatively anti-religious; but in England, where there has co-existed with the Established Church a rival ecclesiastical system, it has been able to make its protest without forsaking Christianity.

As a consequence of this, Toryism, the creed of the

authoritarian, has attracted the political sympathies of the "Church of England party";[1] Liberalism (through its eighteenth-century expression—Whiggism) has successfully wooed the Nonconformists. From the days of Cavalier and Roundhead, when High Anglicans fought Puritans in the Civil War, through the days of the later Stuarts, when Anglican Tories, by Test and Corporation Acts, Schism and Occasional Conformity Acts, tried to undo the work which the Parliamentary struggle and the Toleration Act had accomplished, so that they might destroy the power of their Dissenting-Whig rivals, through the eighteenth century, and on into the nineteenth century, when the Liberal party might almost be described at times as the "Nonconformist conscience" in action, those alliances of Churchman and Tory, Dissenter and Whig have held good.

There is a modern tendency to seek the reasons that govern political allegiances amongst social and economic factors, and to regard men as governed primarily by their economic interests. There can be little doubt that this fashion of thought reflects contemporary conditions. Economics do nowadays play a great part in fashioning political programmes, and politics have become increasingly bound up with economics in an industrialised society. But a historical survey of English party history destroys the illusion that things have been always so. Men live at one and the same time in the "Three Worlds"

---

[1] The Tories made the most of this in the party struggles of Queen Anne's reign. See G. M. Trevelyan, *England under Queen Anne*.

of Religion, Politics, and Economics.[1] Their thoughts in each sphere are modified by ideas from the other two, and, if political thought is now chiefly influenced by economic ideas, it has at various times been correspondingly shaped by elements which were purely religious. The "Three Worlds" are not separated entities; they are three aspects of the life of "Man in Society". They form a unity which is the social life of man, and no historical study, in which any of the three is ignored, can be regarded as complete.

There is, in view of the contemporary economic emphasis, little need to stress the important work of economics in directing the development of English political life since the Industrial Revolution of the eighteenth century. Its influence has been deep and permanent. It has, however, been exerted upon a system already created. English political parties came to birth in a world in which economic factors did not exercise so universal a sway as they do now. Their effect has been one of modification and development, not only of initiation. The genesis of our party system must be sought elsewhere.

English parties have always been divided on the great political issues of "Liberty" or "Authority", "Constitutional and Responsible Government" or "Divine Right", "Civil and Religious Liberty" or "Church and King". These rival political ideals have been capable of affecting the whole outlook of their champions, and this was especially true when they took their origin from the

---

[1] This classification is Professor Ernest Barker's. To him the author owes an inestimable debt of gratitude, for inspiration and encouragement alike.

7

religious ideas inspiring the piety and churchmanship of either side. It is impossible to ascertain in all cases which "World" exerted the prior influence; but there is enough evidence to show that many Englishmen's political allegiances were conditioned by their ecclesiastical prejudices.

If the constitutional conflicts of the first two Stuarts be taken as the first clashes of the historic English parties, it must be admitted that the contest between Puritan and Episcopalian is older than that between Whig and Tory. It was first in the sphere of religion that the Roundhead learned to fight for his cherished liberty. It was in the sphere of religion that the first attack was launched against the all-embracing power of the Elizabethan "Commonwealth". It was from the world of religion that the struggle passed to that of politics.

Medieval reasoning had been coloured by theology, and it had treated all subjects as related to the "Queen of the Sciences". The Reformation rejected much of the teaching of the medieval Church, and, by its individualism, sapped the foundations of the idea of the universal Church. But it did not destroy the theological mould in which men thought. For the authority of the Church it substituted that of the Bible; and the Bible became the greatest force moulding the thought of Englishmen during the period when the embryo parties began to take shape.

The effect of the continual domestic study of the book upon the national character, imagination and intelligence for nearly three centuries to come, was greater than that of any literary movement in our annals, or any religious movement since the coming of St Augustine. New worlds of history and poetry were opened in its pages to a people that had little else to read. Indeed it created the habit of reading and reflection in whole classes of the community and...coloured the daily thought and speech of Britons, to the same degree as they are coloured in our own day by the commonplaces of the newspaper press.[1]

The political parties to which these Bible-reading men of the seventeenth century gave their loyalty were bound to be influenced by their religious ideals. Protestantism had made it possible for private judgment to base rival policies upon the same standard of authority. The English party system was a product of this Protestant legacy, and it derived its greatest force therefrom. The Puritan, who denounced the Established Church and the system of Episcopacy as unscriptural, found in his Bible the divine sanction for his attack upon the constituted authority in either Church or State. It was his theology that made him a Whig. The Tory, who championed his "Church and King", did so as a part of his religion. His inspiration, like that of his political opponent, was that book which supplied his constant thoughts—the Bible. The Bible was the greatest political, as well as the greatest religious dynamic of the seventeenth century.

In France, where Protestantism failed, the Bible never moulded life as it did in England. Men there lacked the religious inspiration of Bible study, which fired the Cromwellians in their struggle against the royal power. They could not appeal, as did the English Puritans, to the intelligent sympathy of a Bible-reading public. The

[1] Trevelyan, *History of England*, p. 367.

9

religious wars in France appeared to the average French-man to be little more than faction fights; the Civil War in England was recognised as a struggle for religious principles, as well as political liberties, a clash of churches as well as of parties. The very ideas of authority and liberty were, to Englishmen, as closely bound up with religion as with politics. The constitutional achievements of the Parliamentary party in the seventeenth century were inspired by the Puritan doctrine of ecclesiastical and spiritual liberty. They were, on its political side, fruits of that religious individualism of which Protestant-ism was the inspiration.

So it came about that English political divisions fol-lowed the divisions between religious individualists and traditionalists. The Puritans struck for ecclesiastical freedom and complete Protestantism; the Anglicans for the Church which they loved, and which they only desired to amend. The Puritans adopted the Protestant doctrine of the "Priesthood of All Believers" and the democratic government of each "Congregation"; the Anglicans retained Catholic doctrines of the ministry, and the traditional hierarchy of Episcopacy. In conse-quence, when constitutional issues arose, it was the Puritans who championed the Parliament, and the Anglicans who fought for the unabated authority of the King. "No King, No Bishop!" (to modify James I's aphorism) represents their position. The issue was joined in the seventeenth century, and, from the resulting struggle, there emerged finally the Whig and Tory parties. Born of ecclesiastical disputes, nurtured amidst religious strife, the two parties, despite their eighteenth-

and nineteenth-century developments, never outgrew
their early religious associations.

The Whig and Tory parties had taken definite shape
by the time Methodism arose. The Nonconformists of
the seventeenth and eighteenth centuries had been Whigs
through the necessity of their own guiding principle and
their struggle for existence; the Methodists, independent
of both Church and Dissent, might ally themselves with
whichever party most adequately expressed their ecclesiastical and political ideals. Eighteenth-century Dissenters had, in the struggle for civil and religious rights,
lost much of the spiritual power which had quickened the
early Puritans, but their battle had been half-won by the
establishment of a Whig party. The Dissenters had spent
themselves in the achievement of political liberty, but
the Methodists were not called upon to make similar
sacrifices. They reaped the fruit of others' sowing and
entered into a heritage for which others had toiled. They
were able to adopt an attitude of isolation from politics
which would not have been possible for the Puritans,
because the Whig party was now prepared to fight the
battle of freedom.

Methodism did in fact affect that attitude of aloofness
from political questions which might be expected of a
society existing for purely religious purposes. Its rapid
and extensive growth, its contact with the affairs of the
world and the social conditions of eighteenth-century
life, and its own modifications of thought and practice,
forced it, however, to take a more active part in public
life. There is always a tendency for religious movements
to produce new political parties, and Professor Élie

Halévy has so assessed the political importance of Methodism:

To this movement, in combination on the one hand with the old Whig political tradition, and on the other with the new ethos produced by the industrial revolution, British Liberalism of the opening XIXth Century owes its distinctive character.[1]

Methodism did not at first accept this political mission. Warned by the spiritual plight of the "Political Dissenters", Wesley had adopted a "No Politics Rule", and had striven to keep his movement out of politics. After he died, his followers carried on this part of his tradition, and, throughout the period covered by this essay, there was no "official" political attitude of the Connexion except one of neutrality. Yet there were within Methodism, even at the time when the "No Politics Rule" was most rigidly enforced, men unwilling to be robbed of their political "birthright", and these were the men who gave a political significance to the new sect.

In the course of the nineteenth century Methodism became the greatest of the Nonconformist Churches, and, in becoming such, it was drawn into the traditional Nonconformist-Liberal alliance. This is not to say that there was any conscious adoption of Liberalism as the political faith of the Methodist Connexions. There was never any public avowal of Liberalism by a Methodist Conference; but it became much more justifiable by the end of the century to assume that a Methodist might be a Liberal than it had been earlier in the period. In the years between 1791 and 1851 the seeds of that develop-

[1] *History of the English People in* 1815, p. 339.

ment were sown. Although during that time it would
have been more accurate to assume that a Methodist
—or at any rate a Wesleyan Methodist—would be a Tory,
there was germinating a new political type of Methodist
Liberal. To trace his genesis down to 1851 must be one
object of this study of the politics of Methodism.

The history of Methodism's relation to politics has
been the story of a Liberal displacement of a strong Tory
sentiment. "Political Quietism" is usually the servant
of Conservatism and of authority, and, in spite of its
non-political intentions, Methodism became a bulwark
of established order, and of the Tory party, in the period
between the Napoleonic Wars and the Reform Bill. The
Whigs had been suspect, because of their sympathy for
the French Revolution, and the Methodists took great
care to clear themselves from any suspicion of complicity
in that movement. Methodism was heartily opposed to
the French Revolution, and its opposition to the Dissenters was in part a reflection of this fear and hatred.
The conservative temper, nurtured by these two factors,
was strengthened by the dominance of a great leader.
Jabez Bunting,[1] who dominated Methodism for half a
century, was politically a Tory, and, whilst preserving
the traditional Methodist attitude of isolation from
politics, he used his influence to discourage Liberal and
Radical elements within the Connexion.

It has been this conservatism which has been most
clearly noticed by outside observers; and it certainly
supplied the predominant political colour of Methodism
in this period. But if the advance of Liberalism was

[1] See Chapter v.

13

comparatively unnoticed, it was none the less real. By 1851 there were two distinct political types in Methodism, one Conservative and one Liberal. Clashes between the two rent the Methodist Church; they also completed Methodism's gravitation towards Non-conformity.

A study of Methodism and politics is really a study in Church history. As the politics of Episcopalians or Puritans reflected their ecclesiastical ideas, so did the politics of Methodists reflect their attitude to problems of Church government. The men most attracted by the Church of England and its tradition of clerical supremacy have been Tories; those inspired by the democratic, anti-clerical notions of Dissent, Liberals. Like the seventeenth-century Nonconformists, Methodists approached questions of politics with minds already influenced by religious ideas. Their prejudices largely determined their attitude to party alignments, and the guiding principle of their political allegiances must be sought in their ecclesiastical doctrines and government.

Methodism did not follow the normal course of Dissenting development either in religion or in politics. It was in both spheres a reaction from the individualism of complete Protestantism.[1] Beginning with a strong authoritarian government under John Wesley himself, it naturally found its political affinities in Toryism. Under the unyielding supremacy of its clerical Conference, it maintained the same position. As it came under the influence of democratic ideas, it drifted from Toryism towards Liberalism. By 1877, when laymen were ad-

[1] See Chapter II.

14

mitted to the "Representative Session" of Conference,[1] the change had taken place. The Liberalism of Hugh Price Hughes at the end of the century, and his Presidency of the first Free Church Council in 1892, were both fruits of the spirit which had gradually transformed both the ecclesiastical and the political character of the Methodism of the nineteenth century.

Its constitutional history is a story of how the elements of authority tried to crush out those of liberty, and of how those elements of liberty resisted that pressure. The various dissensions which tore the Methodist Church between 1797 and 1857[2] received significance from this fact. Because they were manifestations within Methodism of the clash of principles which has shaped the English party system, they must be examined if the basis of Methodist political life is to be appreciated.

The historical problem presented by Methodism's attitude to political matters is of twofold importance. A Church which not only outgrew all the other Dissenting sects, but which was more closely knit together by a system of Connexionalism than they were, a Church which found its greatest strength in industrial districts and amongst members of the middle and working classes, and which, by its conservative temper and its support of established authority, helped to preserve this country from an upheaval such as occurred in France, such a

[1] The Conference of 1878 was the first at which this reform came into effect.
[2] These two dates mark the foundation of the first and the last of the dissentient Methodist Churches: the Methodist New Connexion and the United Methodist Free Churches.

Church was bound, in spite of its professed neutrality, to exert great influence in the political world.

Methodist anxiety to escape suspicion at the time of the French Revolution had strengthened the hold of the government over members of the classes most susceptible to Revolutionary propaganda. The passive resistance of Methodists to the movement for Disestablishment had saved the Church of England from the attack of Radicals and Dissenters. Its ostentatious isolation from party struggles had made of it the useful though unwitting ally of champions of tradition in their war against the encroachments of Democracy. When Methodism was itself changed by the infiltration of democratic ideas, it afforded valuable support to the Gladstonian Liberal party. In the early days, what Methodist political sentiment had existed had been Tory; by the end of the century, probably the majority of Methodist homes contained a portrait of Mr Gladstone. (This was true of the "Minor Methodist" Churches[1] more than of the Wesleyan Connexion, which still retained a strong Conservative tradition.) Whether Tory or Liberal, the influence of a Church so powerful as was Methodism was bound to be considerable, both in local and in national politics.

But, however great was Methodism's influence on the politics of the nineteenth century, its political evolution has a historical importance quite independent of its own activities. The interest of its political relations lies not so much in the part they played in national affairs, as in the way at different times Methodism gave its support to one

[1] By this term is meant those Methodist Churches which originated in the schisms of the nineteenth century.

or other of the historic parties. The study of Methodism
and politics down to 1851 is a study of the religious background of the English party system. It is a study of the
great Dissenting-Whig alliance. Its chief interest lies in
the gravitation of Methodism to that alliance, and not in
any particular features of its own political activity.

If there is more than historical accident and community of interest in the association of Nonconformity
with the Whig-Liberal party—and the championship of
liberty by both of them points to something deeper than
a fortuitous association—a study of Methodism may
reveal it. As Methodism became more Nonconformist,
it became more Liberal. Its desertion from an authoritarian system of Church government, and its progressive
adoption of democratic ideals and a democratic constitution (especially in its "schismatic" branches), were accompanied by a change of political allegiance from Toryism to Liberalism. When Methodism, as a "Reaction in
the Evolution of Protestantism",[1] found little attraction
in either the ecclesiastical or political ideals of Dissent,
and when its government was more authoritarian than
free, its political sympathies were with the Tories. When
it became truly Nonconformist, and shook off its respect
for the Church of England, its politics were inspired by
the same motives as those of the older Dissenters. The
correspondence of the ecclesiastical change with the
political may point to fundamental reasons for the
historic alliance of Nonconformity and Liberalism.

[1] This is le Père Piette's name for Methodism's place in the
history of the Church. His book is entitled *John Wesley: Sa Réaction dans l'Évolution du Protestantisme.*

CHAPTER II

"THE FATHER OF METHODISM": JOHN WESLEY AND THE POSITION OF METHODISM IN THE CHURCH

Christendom was divided at the Reformation into two sections—Catholic and Protestant. In place of one homogeneous Church claiming the allegiance of all Christians in Western Europe, there grew up, beside the truncated Roman Catholic Church, a complex system of national churches, together with churches owning allegiance to neither Pope nor Prince. The new churches were more than societies of men protesting against the rule of the Pope, whether in State or in Church; they were expressions of certain aspects of the Christian faith which had been neglected or underestimated by medieval Catholicism. In the Middle Ages the Church had claimed to be the repository of the whole truth of Christianity; from the time of the Reformation Christian truth was to be expressed partially by both Catholic and Protestant. In place of the one clear light of the medieval Church, there were to be many candles to guide the steps of Christian pilgrims.

The Roman Catholic Church emerged from the struggles of the Reformation as the champion of tradition and authority. With a history unapproachable by any of its rivals, the Roman Catholic Church could appeal from the failures of the present to the glories and revivals of the past, and could give, as an earnest of reform, the evidence of its own vitality. It took its stand upon historical dogmas and creeds; it emphasised the continuity of the life of the Church, and the important corporate aspect of religion; it exalted the hierarchy, and confirmed the supremacy of the Pope; it reaffirmed that the Sacraments of the Church, canonically administered by the ordained priesthood, were the most efficacious "Means of Grace" open to Christians. In all these things Catholicism expressed the authoritarian tradition of the corporate Church.

Against this Catholic tradition the new Protestant Churches appealed to an ideal of liberty. Questioning the dogmatic foundations of Catholic claims, stressing the individual nature of religious experience, rejecting the claims of a priesthood which had arrogated to itself the greatest powers and privileges of the Church, and finding in the Bible alike a final authority and a supreme means of grace, Protestantism rejected the ideals of Catholicism and substituted for them a set of its own. Instead of a corporate and traditional authority, Protestantism strove for the liberty of the individual to read and interpret his Bible by the reasoning of his own enlightened conscience. The appeal from the authority of the Pope to that of the Bible was, however unconscious, essentially an individualistic appeal, for the interpretation put upon the Bible would differ with each individual interpreter.

After the violent changes of the reigns of Edward VI and Mary, the Elizabethan Church Settlement gave to England a Church containing elements both Catholic and Protestant. Elizabeth effected a compromise which rather modified the old Church than made it Protestant. English Protestantism, dissatisfied with the National Church, found expression in Dissenting "Sects". The Church of England retained its old hierarchical organisation, but the sects rejected Episcopacy and all its adjuncts. They developed the individualism of Protestantism, and rejected the plea that the Church should be coterminous with the whole nation. Medieval Christendom had included within its pale almost all but Jews in Western Europe; the Church of England, like Erastian and national Churches elsewhere, claimed to be the "nation on its religious side"; the Dissenting sects regarded the true Church as a society of elect individuals. Theirs was a new ideal of the Church.

The Church of England had been established in the sixteenth century; the sects had developed in the seventeenth; in the eighteenth century came Methodism, and, with Methodism, yet another development of the Reformation. If the Anglican Church had been a reformed Catholic Church, and the Dissenting bodies more logically Protestant, the new Church which was to emerge from the Methodist Revival was different from both. Wesley had inherited from his ancestors traditions both Anglican and Dissenting; consequently the Church which he founded, and which bore upon every part of it the impress of his ideas and personality, came justly to be described as "on the borders of Church and Dissent".[1] It included a great diversity of elements. Essentially Protestant in its reverence for the Bible, in its insistence

[1] Halévy, I, 340.

upon *individual* conversion and responsibility, and in its stress upon Holiness *in* the world,[1] Methodism was yet Catholic in its Sacramentarianism, in its authoritarian government, and in its emphasis upon the necessity of a corporate expression for religious experience. It was indubitably Protestant; but it was a new member of the English Protestant family.

It was a body unlike anything else in English life, and it was unique for three reasons. It could not be satisfactorily classified as a Dissenting body because it was in origin, doctrine, and discipline alike closer to the Church of England than were any of the other sects, and its Anglican connexions were to be a great factor in moulding its outlook upon political questions. The understanding of this "middle position" is of great importance, for much of the misunderstanding from which Methodism has suffered has been due to the failure of observers to realise that, whilst Methodism was obviously more than a mere Anglican Society, it was quite different from the other Dissenting Churches. Its effect on both Anglicanism and Nonconformity was, as Halévy has pointed out, enormous, but Methodism itself was different from both. It was neither hostile nor subservient; it became independent; but its independence was tempered by a filial regard for its Mother Church which tended to make it sympathise rather with the Established Church than with the Dissenting Churches.

If Methodism was unique firstly because of its Anglican sympathies, it was also unique in its doctrine and

[1] See S. G. Dimond, *The Psychology of the Methodist Revival*, p. 242, on this aspect of Methodism.

organisation. Its doctrine, an eighteenth-century delta stream of the perennial evangelical river, has since, to a greater or a less degree, permeated almost every denomination; but its organisation, a creature of eighteenth-century conditions, remains uncopied. Doctrinally, Methodists were severed by their Arminianism from the Calvinist Dissenters, and ecclesiastico-politically, their almost military regimentation under the leadership of John Wesley was a very different thing from the local democracy of Independents and Baptists, and even from the more analogous organisation of Presbyterians.

Herein lay the *fons et origo* of the difference, as of the Church itself. Methodism was the work of a religious genius. If the Church of England had owed its origin to political exigencies, and Puritanism to the influence of uncompromising Protestant ideas coming especially from Geneva, Methodism was the work of one man, and that one man a man of almost unparalleled organising power mingled with vision, energy, force of personality and an implicit and not unreasonable faith that he was an instrument in the hands of God. This was the all-important fact which determined the position of Methodism in the Christian Church.

The life of John Wesley was one of almost unceasing activity. It has been estimated[1] that he travelled 250,000 miles during his evangelistic tours, most of them on horseback over eighteenth-century roads, and that he preached not less than 52,400 times between 1738, when he returned from Georgia, and 1791, when his last sermon was preached eight days before he died.[2] In addition to

[1] *N.H.M.* I, 216.   [2] Piette, p. 545.

this, he read omnivorously, made (and gave away) a fortune from books, sermons, and pamphlets which he either wrote or abridged, kept a journal and a private shorthand diary, carried on a huge correspondence,[1] organised various forms of relief for the poor and unemployed, and had always time to talk or pray with anyone who needed him.

Dr Johnson, who appreciated Wesley's charm, bears ironical witness to his unceasing activity:

John Wesley's conversation is good, but he is never at leisure. He is always obliged to go at a certain hour. This is very disagreeable to a man who loves to fold his legs and have out his talk, as I do.[2]

When in 1753 he was too ill to preach or travel, he began to write his *Notes on the New Testament*, and it was typical of the man that only after he had completed the Deed Poll of 1784 (he was then 81 years old) did he allow himself a holiday in Holland. It was his first holiday in fifty years, and, after it, he returned to his itinerancy.

His untiring physical activity was paralleled by his mental activity. His published works include treatises on almost every branch of human knowledge: theology,

---

[1] See the standard editions of Wesley's *Sermons*, *Journal*, and *Letters*, published by the Epworth Press. His last letter was written on February 24th, 1791 (four days before his death). It was to encourage Wilberforce in his struggle, "like Athanasius *contra mundum*", against "that execrable villainy which is the scandal of the religion of England, and of human nature". His letters and his *Journal* give a lively account of social life in eighteenth-century England, and often his comments upon the state of the roads over which he travelled unceasingly excites comparison with Arthur Young.

[2] Boswell, II, 176.

medicine, science, ancient and modern languages, literature both classical and religious, economics, politics and
social conditions as he continually saw them.[1] Even a
casual reading of his *Journal* must impress one with the
vigour—physical, mental, and spiritual alike—of this
eighteenth-century Oxford don.

The *Journal* contains many references to contemporary political events, and Wesley felt himself, on more than
one occasion, constrained to tender advice on political
matters, both to his own people and to those who were
directly concerned in such struggles as that involved by
the War of American Independence. His interest in and
attitude to politics were those which might be expected
from a man of his class in society. He was an ardent
loyalist and opposed both Jacobites and American malcontents. The wild charges of Jacobitism flung against
him by his opponents, in the hope that they would thereby succeed in inflaming the mob against the Methodists,
appear ludicrous in the light of his own observations.[2] A
High Churchman and a Tory, he was not likely to sympathise with rebels, and his traditional political faith was
perhaps buttressed by his own autocratic tendencies.

W. J. Warner, in *The Wesleyan Movement and the
Industrial Revolution*,[3] notes what he calls the "moral"

[1] Telford, *Life of John Wesley*, p. 385, quotes Green's figures in
the standard work on Wesley bibliography, which give 233 original
works by John Wesley, 100 extracted or edited by him, 8 for which
he wrote a preface or notes, 20 by Charles Wesley alone, and 30
in their joint names.
[2] *Journal*, September 21st, 1745.
[3] Chapter IV, "Political Trends in the Wesleyan Movement",
which contains a much fuller analysis of John Wesley's political
principles than can be attempted here.

and the "theological" aspects of Wesley's theory of the
State, and the deference he accorded to those in authority.
He insisted on the idea of government as a trust, but a
trust from God, not from the people. "The powers that
be are ordained of God", and are therefore to be responsible to God. He had little use for systems of
representation, either of numbers or of property, and,
like Burke, he denied the assumption that a Member of
Parliament was the delegate of his constituency. He did
not preach the divine right of Rotten Boroughs, which
he condemned as "against common sense",[1] but again,
like Burke, he had no faith in the nostrums which
would give power into the hands of a mob, whose unre-
generate violence and stupidity he had bitter cause to
remember.

He may not have perceived the possible clash between
the "moral" and "theological" conceptions of government involved in his thinking, but he was at least consistent in that he found the mainspring of politics in the
responsibility of governors to a supreme God. It was his
belief that only men who were truly religious were fit to be
in authority, and it was at least partly for that reason that
he bade Methodists avoid all bribery and corruption at
election times, and vote for the best man who happened
to be a candidate.[2] He was in politics, as in so many other
spheres, both a realist and an opportunist. He needed
protection against the senseless violence of mobs, and

[1] *Journal*, October 2nd, 1754.
[2] See his *Word to a Freeholder*: "Act as if the whole election
depended on your single vote, and as if the whole Parliament depended
(and therein the whole nation) on that single person whom you now
choose to be a member of it". *Works*, IX, 335.

this protection had to come from the State. He knew at first hand the bigotry and corruption of local magistrates, and he perceived the evils contingent upon elections wherein bribery played such a part as it did in eighteenth-century England,[1] but he believed that necessary reforms could be produced, not by widening the franchise and making it more representative, but alone by regeneration and a sense of duty amongst those in authority. He did not work out all the implications of his theory, and perhaps he overlooked the danger of confusing the actual with the ideal, a danger which besets all metaphysical theorists of the State.

When the radicals called Wesley's attention to the potential threat to English liberties since the " King and Parliament can take them all away ", he replied impatiently, " but they do not; and till it is done Englishmen are free ".[2]

Such was John Wesley's attitude to theoretical difficulties. They appeared to him, as to most men of his class in the eighteenth century, mere political will-o'-the-wisps. It was of greater moment that the English Constitution, as he knew it, secured the substantial benefits of just and peaceful government.

From the different views expressed in his works it might be possible to find evidence in support of theories giving to Wesley almost any political ideal, and it would seem that he might thereby be convicted of inconsistency. Such criticism may be brought to bear upon almost all intelligent and interested observers of national life who

[1] Conference recommended that his *Word to a Freeholder* should be widely distributed in 1767.

[2] Warner, p. 115.

maintain an independent position; but with John Wesley this shortcoming was less important than it might have been with many men. It might even be said that, for the purpose of tracing the genesis of the nineteenth-century Methodist Liberal, John Wesley's political opinions, however interesting, have comparatively little significance.

The influence of Wesley upon social and political conditions in England has been great,[1] but it has worked indirectly. He was naturally interested in politics, but to over-emphasise that interest is to commit a mistake to which political and social historians are prone. He himself said that the mission of Methodism was "to spread Scriptural Holiness throughout the land", and to that end were all his energies bent. He opposed bribery because it lowered the standard of Christian living; he warned members of his Societies to beware lest their participation in politics should make them worldly minded; he disliked disorder and revolution both for their concomitants, and for the way they destroyed that spirit of obedience and order which he valued. Wesley has supplied to many men the inspiration for their social service and political reform, but that inspiration has not come by their study of a "Methodist Ethic", to search for which seems as profitless as to search for the so-called "Christian Ethic". Neither in the pages of the *Works of John Wesley* nor in those of the New Testament can be found a coherent, comprehensive system of politics or

[1] Especially see Halévy on this point. Also Warner, *The Wesleyan Movement and the Industrial Revolution*; J. E. Rattenbury, *Wesley's Legacy to the World*; and Maldwyn Edwards, *John Wesley and the Eighteenth Century*.

political reform. The results achieved by early Christianity and by eighteenth-century Methodism came alike from the working of that Spirit which was the inspiration and the life-force of both.

W. J. Warner's quotation of Leslie Stephen's dictum "that the Methodist movement was essentially moral and philanthropic, but it was cast in a theological mould"[1] betrays a misunderstanding of the position of John Wesley, who would scarcely have endorsed the opinion that

> The revival under Wesley was more of an ethical than a theological movement. It produced important consequences for the political and economic life. It propagated certain definite ideas and attitudes affecting secular activities as part of its normal function. In doing this it undertook to be a real interpretation of the Christian ethic.[2]

One cannot consider philosophical, political, social, or even humanitarian motives to be the basis of the work of a great religious leader, and it is as a religious leader that Wesley has any claim to historical eminence. His thinking, his writing, his social and economic experiments are important as revealing the way he worked out his religion in life, but they are secondary; the primary factor in his work was his evangelism and his organisation of his "United Societies". His monument does not consist of a library of social and economic tracts, but of the greatest Protestant Church in the world, and he must be regarded primarily, not as a social reformer, but as a Churchman.

The approach to the problem presented by the

---

[1] Warner, p. 57.   [2] *Ibid.* p. 56.

Methodist attitude to politics must then be made, not
from outside by a study of the external actions and social
theories professed at any one time by the Church, but,
since Methodism is above all else a *Church*, from the
inside, by an examination of those forces at work within
it determining its outlook. This must be the main line of
thought in the study of conditions determining Methodism's political attitude; social applications of that spirit
must be considered as auxiliary to it.

Here again is a point of difference between Methodism
and the Dissenting sects. It would be unjust to say that
the Dissenters have been equally as interested in politics
as in religion, but in the eighteenth century they had
become deeply involved politically. Methodist politics
were an incidental outcome of conditions; Dissenting
politics were almost inseparably bound up with their own
Church life. It was indeed the realisation of the fate
which had befallen the sects, who had exhausted their
spiritual life in the struggle for freedom, both ecclesiastical and political, that made Wesley and his successors
so careful to warn their people against participation in
politics, and which at least in part explains the "No
Politics" attitude which the Methodist Conference
adopted in the nineteenth century.

If John Wesley's political opinions are of secondary
importance, the more essential aspects of his thought and
his work must be examined more carefully. Both in
doctrine and in ecclesiastical discipline he transmitted to
the Church he founded a system unlike that of any other
Church in England. His originality in both these spheres
must not be overlooked, and the issues involved in this

subject cannot be understood except against the background of the doctrinal and ecclesiastical thought of the founder of Methodism.

Wesley's originality in the sphere of theology has generally been misunderstood both by his panegyrists and by his detractors. Parallels to almost all his ideas may be found elsewhere in the history of dogma, and yet nowhere can be found a parallel to his whole position. That position, which was not the result only of a process of thought, has been described by le Père Piette[1] as "a reaction in the evolution of Protestantism". It is, in many ways, a paradoxical position, and involves a fusion of ideas, which may justifiably be called Catholic, with others quite as incontrovertibly Protestant, of ideas inherited from his Church with others which became real to him as he read and thought, or which suddenly became vivid with the force of revelation. As with his political ideas, it would be a mistake to look for a coherent system of doctrine in the works of John Wesley, and he himself would not have deemed the deficiency of much consequence. On the other hand, it is worth while attempting to trace the origin of some of the ideas he most strongly held, for such an investigation will reveal his true place in the Christian Church,[2] and will make it possible to understand the development of Methodism.

Le Père Piette, a Franciscan friar, with a sympathetic understanding of Wesley's position and work, has em-

[1] In *La Réaction Wesléyenne*.

[2] Dr H. B. Workman's *The Place of Methodism in the Catholic Church* is the best attempt in English to solve this problem and to trace Methodism's connexions with other movements in Christian history.

phasised the Catholic aspect of Wesley's thought, and his revolt against both Lutheranism and Calvinism. He has shown how Wesley's unfortunate experience with the Moravians, who gained the upper hand in the Anglican Societies, such as that at Fetter Lane, drove him into opposition to them, whereas he had previously been an admirer of their discipline and ideas. The doctrine of "Stillness", to which men like Molther gave such a prominent place, led members of the Fetter Lane Society into Antinomianism and into a complete contempt for the ordinances.[1] The *Journal* tells the story of Wesley's attempts to prevent what he felt to be this lapse into heresy, of his failure, and of his eventual resolve to separate himself and his supporters from the Fetter Lane Society and the Moravians in general.[2] From the formation on July 23rd, 1740, of a new Society with twenty-five members who met at the Foundery may be dated the beginning of the "Wesleyan Reaction" which, says Piette, was definitely launched in 1741.[3]

The breach with the Moravians, to whom he had owed so much, demonstrates clearly some of the Catholic elements in Wesley's attitude. One of the characteristics of the "Holy Club" at Oxford had been the importance they had attached to the use of the means of grace, and Wesley's High Churchmanship was opposed to any such

[1] See Wesley's *Journal* for 1740 and J. S. Simon, *John Wesley and the Religious Societies*.

[2] Simon, *John Wesley and the Methodist Societies*, pp. 14–15, points out that the Fetter Lane Society was an Anglican Society while the Wesleys were members of it, and that not until September 7th, 1742, was the Chapel licensed as that of "Moravian Brethren, formerly of the English Communion".

[3] Piette, p. 517.

disregard for Catholic usage as was made quite explicit by "the Germans", who rejected the sacraments as "Works". In his insistence upon the value of the sacraments Wesley was indeed more Catholic than were either the Anglicans or the Nonconformists of his day. The work of Laud and Andrewes in the Church of England had not been developed by the Bishops of the Restoration and Hanoverian periods, and the " Holy Club " at Oxford had added to their unpopularity by regular attendance at Holy Communion. Both as an "ordinance" and as a traditional vehicle of grace, Wesley prized the sacraments, and he regarded them with a reverence not inferior to that of the members of another Oxford Movement in the next century.[1]

In yet another way does this breach with the prophets of " Stillness " illustrate John Wesley's divergence from the general Protestant individualist tradition. The Moravians carried their individualism to such extremes that there was for them no place for Wesley's conception of the Church with its continuous corporate life and its sacraments. The doctrine of " Stillness " was incipiently anarchist, and the man who held that "the Bible knows no such thing as solitary religion" had little patience with religious anarchism. It was this which made him so unjust in his adverse opinions of mysticism.[2] His love of order and hatred of "enthusiasm" were essentially Catholic, for by enthusiasm he meant religious indi-

[1] For a comparison between Methodism and the Oxford Movement, especially concerning the sacraments, see Rattenbury, Chapter XVI.
[2] Workman, *The Place of Methodism in the Catholic Church*, § VI, pp. 77–87.

vidualism without respect for the Bible or for the Church and its means of grace.[1]

But if his love of order and his emphasis upon the social aspect of religion were Catholic, his opportunist use of any means of preaching or of furthering his work were much more in line with Protestant ideas. He respected authority and tradition, only in so far as they did not interfere with what he conceived to be his work. He was quite Protestant in his reverence for the Bible, which, from the beginning, was taken as the "sufficient rule of life for the Methodists". The teaching of the New Testament in particular was the criterion whereby both doctrines and systems of Church government were to be tested. Most definitely of all, his emphasis upon "Experience", which may be taken as the constitutive element in his doctrine, meant giving to creeds and dogmas a position inferior to that in which any orthodox Catholic must have placed them.

That his doctrinal system contained elements drawn from such diverse sources was perhaps the result of his strong individuality, but it was also the result of his object in life, and his dogmatic position was very largely the outcome of the problems he had to face and the circumstances under which he had to work. Cherished inherited beliefs had to be modified, recognised methods discarded, new truths accepted, new instruments forged, as his work proceeded. To the accomplishment of that work, all else was to be subservient. It was in this opportunism, this "pragmatism"—Piette[2] calls him a "Pragmatist before the term was invented"—which led

[1] There are many examples of this in the *Journal*.   [2] p. 595.

to differences of opinion with his more conservatively High Church brother, Charles, who disapproved of much that John felt he was driven to do.

It was indeed in this pragmatism that Wesley's originality lay. He cannot justly be described as belonging to any one school of Christian thought. Had he followed Butler and Berkeley in their intellectual onslaught upon the prevalent Deism of their age, he might have kept his thought more consistent, but, although he did not despise intellect—his use of the pen has caused his comparison with Wyclif,[1] and he had no respect for those who would have minimised the part which might be assigned to thought in religion—he had made up his mind to preach "the simple truth for simple folk".[2] That "simple truth" was not bound up with any theological system as such, but was based upon the peculiarly Wesleyan doctrine of "Assurance".

As an Arminian he believed in the possible salvation of every soul, and in the responsibility of each soul to God. He rejected the "stern decrees" of Calvinist orthodoxy as inconsistent with the love of God. With the Lutherans he agreed as to the necessity of "Faith" whereby alone men might be justified, but he rejected Luther's violent "Solifideianism" which so easily produced Antinomians, and he quarrelled with the Moravians when they held that there were no "degrees in faith". Doctrinally, in fact, the first "Conference", held in 1744, stated Methodism's position as one different alike from that of Rome, Luther, or Calvin, though

[1] Workman, *op. cit.* pp. 72–4.
[2] Preface to his *Sermons* published in 1747.

it scarcely laid down any positive system. "Justification" was by faith, and to be justified meant "to be pardoned and received into God's favour, and into such a state that, if we continue therein, we shall be finally saved";[1] the assurance of justification was held to be conscious, and good works, both before and after it, were enjoined as essential. At the same Conference the question of "Sanctification", which was the perfecting of the state initiated by justification, was considered, and the opinions expressed here were much more guarded.[2] It is significant that, although Wesley preached "Christian Perfection", he never for himself laid claim to its attainment, and, though he never ceased to regard it as an urgent need, he was, as he grew older, increasingly cautious of preaching its logical implications. The findings of this first Conference at City Road illuminate the mind of Wesley and reveal alike his grasp of essentials, and his caution in dealing with disputed or undeveloped truths.

An understanding of this cautious attitude to matters of doctrine is important. It explains why Wesley never instituted for his Societies any doctrinal standard or set of Articles. He never intended to be an innovator, and he believed that all his doctrines could be brought within the meaning of the Thirty-nine Articles. It was perhaps the elasticity of these Articles that hid from him the magnitude of that "reaction in the evolution of Protestantism", which it enabled him to bring about, and the

[1] See the Bennet "Minutes" of the first Conference (W.H.S. Publications, No. 1), p. 8.
[2] *Minutes of Conference of* 1744, pp. 11–12.

3-2

accomplishment of which was to be his life-work. In his *Character of a Methodist*,[1] an apologetic pamphlet written to enlighten a curious and often hostile public as to the real nature of Methodism, he took care to stress the fact that Methodism was not bound up with any body of doctrines, but was the essence of Christianity. Orthodoxy on matters of secondary importance was to John Wesley, and has generally been to Methodism as a whole, of comparatively little moment. His views on "Salvation" are interesting as showing his catholicity and freedom of thought:

Being alone in the coach, I was considering several points of importance: and thus much appeared as clear as the day:

That a man may be saved who cannot express himself properly concerning imputed righteousness. Therefore to do this is not necessary to salvation.

That a man may be saved who has not clear conceptions of it: (yea, that never heard the phrase). Therefore clear conceptions of it are not necessary to salvation; yea it is not necessary to salvation to use the phrase at all.

That a pious Churchman who has not clear conceptions even of justification by faith, may be saved; therefore clear conceptions even of this are not necessary to salvation.

That a Mystic who denies justification by faith (Mr Law, for instance), may be saved. But if so, what becomes of "Articulus stantis vel cadentis ecclesiae"? If so, is it not high time for us "Projicere ampullas et sesquipedalia verba"? and to return to the plain word, "He that feareth God, and worketh righteousness, is accepted with Him".[2]

[1] Published in 1742, *Works*, VIII, 340–7.
[2] *Journal*, December 1st, 1767. Lord Acton found here the point of separation between Methodism and the Church of England. The events of 1784, he considered, but actualised a position spiritually implicit since 1767. (Quoted *C.M.H.* VI, 85–6.)

In such a passage he was disagreeing with attempts to stereotype the way of God's working, and, if his words reveal the modifications he had introduced into his òwn doctrines of justification, assurance, and the "New Birth", they reveal too the importance he attached to the work of common sense guided by the Spirit of Truth. His legacy to his Church contained a tolerance of difference of opinion and an elasticity of creed, which, whilst bringing into Methodism many of the treasures of the Holy Catholic Church, has enabled his Church the more readily to accept new truth.[1] That legacy included a sacramental and a High Church element along with a rejection of what he felt to be the spurious claims of Episcopalians or "Solifideianists"; an exalted conception of the Bible as the inspired Word of God, together with a habit of interpreting it in the light of a man's Christian experience; an individualism which made the salvation of a man's soul and the holiness of his life his chief end, together with an emphasis upon righteousness in all his dealings with others; justification by faith alone, and rigorous insistence upon the production of the "Fruits of the Spirit". All these John Wesley bequeathed to Methodism; and by means of these, he built up a Church not only on the borders of Anglicanism and Nonconformity, but also nearer to the "right wing" of Protestantism than he realised—and certainly nearer than many of his followers have since cared to admit.

[1] Whilst there has been conservatism and even obscurantism in the attitude of Methodists towards new truth, the absence of any *rigid* formularies has allowed a silent revolution to be worked within a Church in which wellnigh all shades of Christian opinion are now "comprehended".

Piette's classification, even doctrinally considered, points to elements in the Methodism of John Wesley all-important for the understanding of its development and modification in the following century.

If one turns from matters of doctrine to matters of Church government, the special position of Methodism in the Church is even more clearly revealed. No other Church has ever been so organised, because no other Church has been founded in the same way. In almost every branch of its organisation it has combined auto-cracy with at least incipient democracy.[1] This powerful organisation has, with modifications, lasted from Wesley's day to the present; it has been the cause of the various dissensions which tore nineteenth-century Methodism, and it has helped to determine that peculiar attitude which Methodists have adopted towards political questions and principles.

It is in matters of Church government that Churchmen most closely approach the sphere of political ideas, and it is hard to escape from the conclusion that most of the training of Methodists in abstract political ideas came from the quarrels over ecclesiastical administration within their own churches. Such a fact cannot be overlooked when dealing with the nineteenth-century Methodist and his political alliances. The constitutional history of Methodism was closely bound up with the history of its members' politics. It is sufficient to note the fact here, so that the importance of an understanding of

[1] Both Warner and Edwards notice "latent Liberalism" in eighteenth-century Methodism, and this fact may strengthen their contention.

Wesley's ecclesiastical machine and its working may be appreciated.

John Wesley's organising ability has been compared with that of both Ignatius Loyola and Cardinal Richelieu, and he deserves a high place in ecclesiastical history as a church organiser alone. During his fifty years' active, itinerant leadership of the "Reaction", he was the undoubted head of the movement. The universal love and respect of his followers were his, and he was able to hold the reins of authority without serious challenge from any rival. Not only was he in a position to exercise this power, but he did so; and, in spite of the rapid spread of the movement, and the vast amount of evangelism and writing he had to do, he was himself largely responsible for the work of organisation. He laid down rules for the ordering of Connexional concerns, and he wielded decisive influence in the local affairs of all the Societies he visited constantly in the course of his itinerancies. He was the architect and builder of Methodism; its strength was the result of his work, and its idiosyncrasies were the reflection of his.

His coadjutors were of two kinds: clergymen of the Church of England, and laymen he recruited as the work demanded their services. This division of his fellow-workers was of importance; for, although he was the leader of both, he was, amongst his brother-clerics, *primus inter pares*, whereas to his lay helpers he was a captain. In like manner the ordained clergy amongst his helpers formed a kind of aristocracy, and to them were allowed privileges forbidden to the lay "Assistants", "Helpers", and "Local Preachers". They alone might administer the sacraments, since they alone had been canonically ordained (Wesley never forsook this belief, and when he broke with the Church in ordaining preachers for Methodist service both at home and overseas, he did so on the grounds of expediency, and because he held that New Testament teaching gave to Presbyters an equal right of ordination with that historically accorded to Bishops).[1] In this matter Wesley's aristocratic leanings fortified what was also demanded by the exigencies of leading the revival. Men like his brother Charles and the eccentric Grimshaw of Haworth, Perronet, Whitefield, Venn, Fletcher of Madeley and others, rendered invaluable service to the cause of Methodism, and were fitted by their education and habitual practice to be leaders and overseers. Without the help of this handful of enthusiastic Anglican clergymen, John Wesley's work would have been both harder and of a different kind, for the effectiveness of a movement depends much on the quality of its leadership.

W. J. Warner, in his chapter on "The Bias of Wesleyan Leadership",[2] examines the classes from which Wesley drew his assistants and helpers, his local preachers and "Class Leaders", and notes how they were chosen by methods of natural selection, in that men who were obviously fitted to hold the respect of their fellows came to exercise these posts of responsibility in the Societies. That Methodism's leaders were "thrown up" rather than "imposed" is true—in a movement so wide-

[1] He was "in spite of the violent prejudice of his education" influenced in this by Lord King's *Account of the Primitive Church* which he read in 1746. *Journal*, January 20th, 1746.
[2] Chapter VIII.

spread it could not be avoided—but it was not simply the presence of Anglican clergy in the ranks that prevented the ministers being regarded as the servants of the people, even though they might have been recruited from the Societies. Democracy might nominate, but it was not allowed to command, or even to appoint, its ministers. No man might "travel" without the direct approbation of Wesley, and the assistants and helpers were responsible, not to their flocks, but to their leader, who in 1768 forbade his itinerant preachers to combine their old occupations with their preaching in the way that the local preachers continued to do.

He strove to visit all his Societies at least once a year, and his visits generally involved a review of local affairs. He expelled or accepted members, appointed local preachers or confirmed the appointments of those who had begun to preach without his express sanction. If he was dissatisfied with such men, he rejected them, and, whilst he respected the opinion of those with local knowledge of the men and conditions he was examining, he reserved to himself the absolute right to decide on all disputed points. He examined candidates for the itinerancy, and decided whether or not they should be allowed to take part with that band of preachers to whom above all fell the work of spreading the gospel of the revival. Amongst all who were his fellow-workers, John Wesley himself was the undoubted head, and he exercised supreme discretionary and visitatorial powers over all the "People called Methodists".

Methodism spread not only where the word of the itinerants was proclaimed, but spontaneously wherever there were Methodists. Many of the Societies owed their origin to being directly founded by John Wesley or one of his preachers, on a plan influenced by the old Anglican Religious Societies, but a great many others grew, in a manner akin to that of the early Church, around single Methodists or small groups possessed of a missionary spirit. Wesley acted like Paul in this movement, giving advice, regulating the government of the Societies, and, when he visited them, commanding them in the same way as he commanded the Societies he had himself founded. Where his authority was concerned there was no distinction. The Methodist Societies were, as he called them, "United Societies", and their unity was made a reality by his headship. It is a feature of eighteenth-century Methodism that recalls the intention of the Oath of Salisbury in 1086.[1] This personal allegiance to him was the cement which first made of these scattered groups of men and women a strongly organised Church, with a firm Connexional system of government. It was a cement which hardened until it became an integral part of the fabric of Methodism. The "hardening process" was akin to that which took place in the early Church. It has been repeated in modern times by the growth of "Native" Churches which, at first dependent on missionaries, have become definite entities with their own life and $\mathring{\eta}\theta o\varsigma$.

[1] By which William the Conqueror reserved to himself, as King, the right to call upon every free man, whoever his feudal lord might be, to bear arms in his service. The Oath of Salisbury and the policy it exemplified bound English feudalism to the King as Continental feudalism was not bound. Wesley applied the same principle of a personal bond between the leader and his followers.

The system of Methodism, with its "Classes" and "Bands" (which have since died out), its "Circuits", "Synods", and "Conference", has sometimes been characterised as a system of Fellowship, by its very nature potentially democratic. There is in this view a great deal that is true. Methodism tended to be equalitarian, and men of different social grades met in the same classes and Church meetings. It has been no uncommon thing throughout Methodist history for workmen to be their employers' class leaders, and the comparative rarity of Methodist members of the upper classes may partially account for this phenomenon. But this social equality does not necessarily imply a democratic form of government, and an examination of John Wesley's Methodism reveals the fact that its organisation was far from being democratic.

When the growth of the work obviously demanded delegation of power to people in areas in which Wesley himself could only exercise visitatorial authority, he still retained his final right of decision, and he himself appointed the men who should be class leaders. That he should have taken it upon himself to appoint the office-holders in Methodism, from the itinerant preachers down to the trustees of his Chapels, and the stewards and the class leaders of his Societies, is a witness to his grasp of detail and his aim of centralisation. Democracy implies representative government; representative government was a conception foreign to the mind of Wesley. His letter to John Mason,[1] written when he had only another year to live, shows that he had

[1] January 13th, 1790.

no intention of slackening the grip he had held all his life:

My dear Brother,

As long as I live, the people shall have no share in choosing either Stewards or Leaders among the Methodists. We have not, and never had, any such custom. We are no republicans, and never intend to be. It would be better for those who are so minded to go quietly away.[1] I have been uniform both in doctrine and discipline for above these fifty years; and it is a little too late for me to turn into a new path now I am grey-headed....

Such were the views of John Wesley on democracy and the cult of representation. He was a paternalist in matters of government all through the half-century when Methodism was organised, and he stamped his personality upon every part of the machine he made.

The most peculiarly Methodist institution in the whole system was the annual Conference, which was first called in 1744.[2] It was the central point of the Church's organisation and formed Wesley's "consilium". Its name gives an idea of its true purpose. It was a body which should consider the needs of the Societies, and advise Wesley upon the course he should steer. It was composed entirely of itinerant preachers, whose only right to be present was the receipt of an invitation from Wesley himself. More than anything in Methodist organisation "Conference" is an example of Wesley's military com-

[1] Wesley's comparative indifference to numbers in his Societies is noteworthy. He ruthlessly pruned his Societies of any whom for any reason he felt to be undesirable members.
[2] The Minutes of the first five Conferences have been published (as their first publication) by the Wesley Historical Society.

mand of affairs, and it is also an example of the way his expedients became parts, not merely of the *bene esse*, but of the *esse* of the Church. This "Council of War", with its freedom of discussion and advisory functions, became, after Wesley's death, the sovereign power of Methodism. Jabez Bunting could appeal to it as to the "living Wesley"; it certainly came to regard itself as "Wesley in Commission".

John Wesley's *Apologia* in 1766, when he feared, owing to an accident, that he might not see another Conference, is a sufficient comment upon the design involved in holding Conference, and also upon his supreme power. It reveals his attitude to Church government, and his resolve to remain master in what had always been his own house:

In 1744 I wrote to several clergymen, and to all who then served me as sons in the Gospel,[1] desiring them to meet me in London[2] to give me their advice concerning the best method of carrying on the work of God. They did not desire this meeting: but I did, knowing that "in a multitude of counsellors there is safety". And when their number increased, so that it was neither needful nor convenient to invite them all, for several years I wrote to those with whom I desired to confer, and these only met at the place appointed; till at length I gave a general permission, that all who desired it might come. Observe!—I myself sent for these, of my own free choice; and I sent for them to advise, not govern me. Neither did I at any of those times divest myself of any part of that power above described, which the providence of God had cast upon me, without any design or choice of mine.

[1] I.e. the assistants or itinerant preachers.
[2] At the old Foundery in City Road—the "Mother Church of Methodism".

What is that power? It is a power of admitting into, and excluding from the societies under my care: of choosing and removing stewards; of receiving or of not receiving helpers;[1] of appointing them when, where, and how, to help me; and of desiring any of them to meet me, when I see good. And as it was merely in obedience to the providence of God, and for the good of the people, that I at first accepted this power, which I never sought,—nay, a hundred times laboured to throw off—so it is on the same considerations, not for profit, honour, or pleasure, that I use it at this day. But several gentlemen are much offended at my having so much power. My answer to them is this:

"I did not seek any part of this power; it came upon me unawares. But when it was come, not daring to bury that talent, I used it to the best of my judgement; yet I never was fond of it. I always did, and do now, bear it as my burden; the burden which God lays upon me, and therefore I dare not yet lay it down." But if you can tell me any one, or any five men, to whom I may transfer this burden, who can and will do just what I do now, I will heartily thank both them and you.

But some of our helpers say, "This is shackling free-born Englishmen", and demand a free Conference: that is, a meeting of all the preachers, wherein all things should be determined by most votes.

I answer,—"It is possible, after my death, something of this kind may take place; but not while I live. To me the preachers have engaged themselves to submit, to serve me as sons in the Gospel. But they are not thus engaged to any man, or number of men besides. To me the people in general will submit. But they will not yet submit to any other".

It is nonsense, then, to call my using this power, "shackling free-born Englishmen". None needs to submit to it, unless

[1] Note how the names "Assistant" and "Helper" imply Wesley's supremacy. Their later names were "Superintendents" and "Travelling Preachers".

he will; so there is no shackling in the case. Every preacher and every member may leave me when he pleases. But while he chooses to stay, it is on the same terms that he joined me at first.

"But this is arbitrary power; this is no less than making yourself a Pope."

If by arbitrary power you mean a power which I exercise singly, without any colleagues therein, this is certainly true; but I see no hurt in it. Arbitrary, in this sense, is a very harmless word. If you mean unjust, unreasonable, or tyrannical, then it is not true.

As to the other branch of the charge, it carries no face of truth. The Pope affirms that every Christian must do all he bids, and believe all he says, under pain of damnation. I never affirmed anything that bears any, the most distant resemblance to this. All I affirm is, "The preachers who choose to labour with me, choose to serve me as sons in the Gospel";—and "the people who choose to be under my care, choose to be so on the same terms they were at first".

Therefore, all talk of this kind is highly injurious to me who bear this burden merely for your sakes. And it is exceedingly mischievous to the people, tending to confound their understandings, and to fill their hearts with evil surmisings and unkind tempers towards me, to whom they really owe more, for taking all this load upon me—for exercising this very power—for shackling myself in this manner,—than for all my preaching put together. Because preaching twice or thrice a day is no burden to me at all; but the care of all the preachers and all the people, is a burden indeed.[1]

This explanation of his position is not belied by an appeal to the facts of his life. He believed himself called of God to the work of spreading and organising Methodism, and his grasp of authority was never a selfish grasp.

---

[1] *Minutes of Conference of 1766*, I, 61–2.

He was a man of real humility; but he was not blinded by false modesty to a realisation that he alone could do the work to which he had been called. Such conviction might produce jealousy amongst lesser men—and it did—but the mass of Methodists, both amongst the preachers and the people, knew that John Wesley was not mistaken in this estimate of his own abilities.

The greatest enemy of a "benevolent despot"—and Wesley lived in the age of benevolent despots—is usually himself. He tends to become "an old man in a hurry", and to be forced by circumstances, and the proximity of his own death, to try to bring his policy prematurely to fruition. An old man who is uncertain of his successors cannot sow the seeds of his policy in patience; he must attempt to finish the work that was given him to do. Especially is this true in a case where, as with Wesley, an adequate successor is not to be found.

Wesley realised this difficulty, but he did not let it worry him. The death of Fletcher of Madeley in 1785 and of Charles Wesley in 1788 destroyed whatever hopes men might have had that any one man would take John Wesley's place, but by the "Deed Poll" of 1784 he had anticipated the difficulty. This Chancery Deed[1] gave a legal description of "the Conference of the people called Methodists". It was to be composed of one hundred appointed travelling preachers (the "Legal Hundred"),[2] and was to be made the chief ecclesiastical authority in the Connexion. The reign of the benevolent despot was

[1] Text in *N.H.M.* II, Appendix B.
[2] The "Legal Hundred" ceased to exist when Methodist Union was accomplished in 1932.

to end with the "Father[1] of Methodism". He had not failed; his work was done; and the organisation he had built up lasted on after his death. It has been modified by the events of the nineteenth century, but it has never quite lost the shape into which John Wesley moulded it.

It may now be possible to estimate the position of this "Reaction in the Evolution of Protestantism" in relation to Anglicanism and Dissent, and to realise the force of this description of eighteenth-century Methodism. The work of a man so strongly individualistic as Wesley could not easily be assimilated by the National Church of the day, however much he might protest that he did not wish to break away from the Church; nor could Societies, owing their inspiration and organisation to so strong a Churchman as Wesley, be simply classed as Nonconformist Conventicles. The opposition of the English Bench of Bishops, and George III's refusal to allow the ordination of any Bishops for work amongst the recalcitrant colonists, had led Wesley, who could not complacently watch the work of God crippled by however regrettable a quarrel between the King and his subjects, to ordain his own Superintendents and Bishops for America.[2] Wesley's work had become more than national,

---

[1] At Wesley's funeral service the word "Father" was substituted spontaneously for the word "brother" in the reading of the service by Richardson, a preacher of 30 years' standing—Southey, p. 342.

[2] He ordained Coke and Asbury in 1784, "to be joint Superintendents over our brethren in North America". In 1785–6 he ordained Superintendents for Scotland and Ireland; and in 1787, 1788, and 1789 for England also. These men were ordained as Presbyters, but in North America, in the absence of Anglican Bishops, they took the style of "Bishop". Elsewhere the Superintendents were never called Bishops.

and, however patriotic he might feel, his work could brook no mere national or political obstruction. The date of the Deed of Declaration and of the ordinations for America (1784) may be taken as the date of the *practical* breach of John Wesley with the Church of England. It was a breach forced on him only by the conditions under which he had had to work, by the unsympathetic policy of the English Bishops, and by the world-wide nature of Wesley's influence. Nevertheless it was a real breach. That he could not use his Societies to strengthen the Church of England was one of Wesley's greatest disappointments. The ordinations and the Deed Poll show that he realised in part the failure of this ideal, but as late as 1788 he was talking about "living and dying a member of the Church of England". Such was the wistful cry of a prophet not without honour save in his own communion. He loved the Church; but his work was of more importance even than the Church.

Wesley left in England a new religious force, theologically antipathetic to the Calvinist Dissenters, suspect to and rejected by the Church of England, but organised to become a powerful influence both in its own sphere, and in its relations with the other parties. He had been careful always to stress the idea that Methodism was really the constitutive element in all true religion and that a man's ecclesiastical opinions were of secondary importance. He had rejoiced that the spread of Methodism had increased the numbers of communicants at the parish churches,[1] but he had never insisted that Dissenters

---

[1] E.g. at Huddersfield where Henry Venn was Vicar. Simon, *John Wesley, the Master Builder*, p. 104.

should change their allegiance when they joined his Societies. Membership of the "United Societies" was intended to be supplementary to ordinary Church membership.[1] He said in 1788:

There is no other religious Society under heaven, which requires nothing of men in order to their admission into it, but a desire to save their souls. Look all around you, you cannot be admitted into the Church or Society of the Presbyterians, Anabaptists, Quakers, or any others, unless you hold the same opinions with them, and adhere to the same mode of worship. The Methodists alone do not insist on your holding this or that opinion, but they think and let think. Neither do they impose any particular mode of worship, but you may continue to worship in your former manner, be it what it may. Now I do not know any other religious Society, either ancient or modern, wherein such liberty of conscience is now allowed or has been allowed since the age of the Apostles! Here is our glorying; and a glorying peculiar to us! What Society shares it with us?[2]

Such was John Wesley's ideal; but when catholicity of appeal was wedded to an iron organisation, the result was the birth of a new Church which bore the characteristics of both its parents. The revival lived on after Wesley's death, but it was embodied, no longer in a federation of "United Societies", but in a Church, and that Church was modified by the events of the nineteenth century in such a way that, as Piette remarks, the "Wes-

[1] The Societies, like the older religious societies, met out of Church hours, which were then morning and afternoon. It was because of Methodist competition, which had annexed the evening, that the Church of England moved its services to the evening also.
[2] *Journal*, May 18th, 1788. Compare also the latter part of *The Character of a Methodist*.

4-2

leyan Reaction" perished, and Methodism became the largest of the Nonconformist bodies.

It was not so in the eighteenth century. The Anglican Church embodied the sixteenth-century ideal of the Church as institutional, and as the universal Church of the whole nation; the sects embodied the seventeenth-century ideal of the Church as individualist and exclusive, in that it consisted of a Communion of Saints, called out from the world, the "elect" of Puritan theology; Methodism gave a new eighteenth-century interpretation of the Church, combining a voluntary principle with authoritarian government, an individualist and Puritan basis of salvation, with a universal application of the doctrine. The position of Methodism in the Christian Church was a new position, because it involved a new conception of the Church. It was the result of Wesley's genius for what Piette calls "organising his converts in the fervour of the Christian life".[1]

From a political point of view the position of this new Church was of great importance. The Church of England was traditionally Tory, the sects traditionally Whig, but Methodism's position remained doubtful. Like a piece of steel between two magnets it was pulled either way, and, although John Wesley's example in keeping Methodism out of party politics was followed by the Conference, circumstances forced its members into more and more active participation in that forbidden sphere. The part that Methodism played in nineteenth-century politics was conditioned by its place in English religious life.

In the study of this question Wesley's own political

[1] *Op. cit.* p. 648.

52

opinions are of comparatively little importance; his ecclesiastical opinions are all-important, for they produced
the framework within which the nineteenth-century
Methodists' political thinking was done. John Wesley
had been a Tory and a High Churchman. "His High
Churchmanship was modified because it interfered with
his work, his Toryism was subject to no such strain, and
remained unaltered."[1] After his death, in the welter of
ideas produced by the French Revolution, his followers
were to find both the ecclesiastical system and the political
ideas which he had left them subjected to a strain which
modified both. The events of those years revealed that it
was the religious work of the founder of Methodism
which was to be less shaken, and which was to condition
the political thinking of his disciples.

[1] Edwards, p. 14.

CHAPTER III

LIBERAL DEVELOPMENTS AND THE METHODIST NEW CONNEXION, 1791–97

The early ministry of John Wesley had been regarded by his fellow-clergymen either with indifference or with a hostility not always veiled. He himself was subjected to ridicule, calumny, misrepresentation, and, more than once, physical violence, whilst his Societies had to undergo all kinds of persecution.[1] Towards the end of his life, his success, his patent sincerity, his common sense and skill as a controversialist, and, from a governmental point of view, his reiterated political rectitude, brought about a change in public opinion. Hostility and opposition remained, but persecution slackened, and Wesley's visitations of his United Societies began to wear the aspect of triumphal progresses.

When he died in 1791, Methodism consisted of about 136,000 members, of whom about 72,000[2] were members of Societies in Great Britain. In addition to these *members*, who had been enrolled in "classes", and who accepted the word of John Wesley as their ecclesiastical law, there were many more "adherents", whose numbers have been estimated[3] at about 800,000 (500,000 in Great Britain), and who had been affected by Methodist preaching although they had not joined the classes. The appeal

[1] See the earlier part of John Wesley's *Journal*, and *Lives of the Methodist Preachers*, passim. The Hobill Collection of pamphlets contains a good selection of *Attacks on Methodism*.
[2] 71,568 in 1790.   [3] *N.H.M.* I, 368–9.

of Methodism was wide in its scope, but it kept its privileges of membership only for those who were ready to accept also the responsibilities of its fellowship. Continual absence from class involved a loss of membership, and consequently the number of members remained small as compared with the number of those who had been affected by Methodism, and who attended its Sunday services.

The geographical distribution of the Methodist Societies had been largely determined by certain conditions of eighteenth-century life. Not only was the Church of England lacking in zeal; it was most inelastically organised. The chaos of Parliamentary representation in the eighteenth century was paralleled by the state of the parishes. Parishes were most unevenly scattered about the country, and grave anomalies existed. Kent was full of parishes; Lancashire had about forty in all. Many of the growing industrial towns in Lancashire were served from the adjacent villages,[1] and in many of them no churches were built during the time when their population was increasing at an unprecedented rate. Halifax was a huge parish covering more than a hundred square miles, and the most conscientious clergyman would have

[1] Liverpool was for long a part of the parish of Walton. Oldham (the author's native town) was a parochial chapelry in the parish of Prestwich-cum-Oldham. Its parish Church of St Mary (though not the present building) has existed since the thirteenth century, but, whilst St Peter's and Hollinwood churches were built in 1765, no other churches were built until St James's, Greenacres, in 1829, and then Christ Church, Glodwick, in 1844. There is a Methodist Chapel dating from Wesley's visit in 1790. The neglect of Oldham by the Established Church in the late eighteenth century was typical of its treatment of other similar towns. The results were to be important in the nineteenth century.

found it impossible to satisfy the spiritual needs of a
population rapidly growing throughout an area of this
size. In Cornwall the churches had been built where the
hermits had once lived, and consequently many of them
were far from the villages dependent upon them. In
Lincolnshire the people had churches, but no clergy,
for the clergy usually lived in the cathedral town.
Pluralities and absenteeism were general, and not until
the Clergy Residence Act of 1803 was anything done to
reform these abuses.[1]

Into this world of inefficiency, inelasticity, and complacent torpor, came the restless energy of Methodist
evangelism. But the new movement was led by a man
who was a clergyman of the Church of England, and who
was anxious not to weaken his Church. For a long time
he regarded his Societies as auxiliaries to the Established
Church, and, as a rule, he did not try to set up Societies
in those places which were already served by an efficient
Parish Church. The advice he gave to his "Helpers"
was the rule he adopted for himself:

> You have nothing to do but to save souls. Therefore, spend
> and be spent in this work; and go always not only to those
> who want you, but to those who want you most[2].

The application of this principle led Wesley to go to
districts where the Church, either through indifference,
or through bad organisation, had failed to meet the
spiritual needs of the people. Kingswood, near Bristol,

[1] Sydney Smith felt himself hardly treated when the passing of
this Act compelled him to leave London and "go into exile" in his
parish. See Hesketh Pearson, *The Smith of Smiths*, p. 141.
[2] Wesley's *Twelve Rules of a Helper*, No. 11.

was perhaps the best example of this; but it was equally true of Cornwall, the Black Country, the new industrial towns of Lancashire and Yorkshire, and the north-east coast.

The "Assistants" and helpers whom he appointed to the work carried on his policy. They were able, in the England of Hogarth's *Gin Lane*, and amongst the half-savage miners and operatives of the north, midlands, and west, to find converts not much more civilised than the negroes whom the nineteenth century set out to evangelise. The Methodist preachers found here the greatest need, and, after some rebuffs, the readiest and most permanent response. There seemed little need to compete with the Establishment when there were so many people in Britain untouched by any form of the Gospel. It was here that the greatest civilising work of Methodism was done. In Cornwall, to take but one example, a people notorious for smuggling and its attendant evils, was converted by Wesley and his Societies[1] into a sober, law-abiding, Sabbatarian race, whilst, in the north and midlands, Methodism was a powerful factor in the production of that self-reliant working class which was to be so important in nineteenth-century politics. Their religion civilised these northern artisans as well as inspired them.

Methodism had done a work which the inelasticity of Anglican organisation had prevented the Established Church from doing. The centralised control of John Wesley provided a far more efficient instrument of evangelism and organisation than did the hide-bound system

---

[1] No smuggler might remain a member of any of Wesley's Societies.

of eighteenth-century Episcopacy. By the time the Church of England had awakened to the necessity for its own reform, the work of Methodism had become established. When, at last, some effort was made by the Government to remedy the deficiency, the grip of the Methodists upon the new industrial areas presented a serious problem. The letter of the Mayor of Liverpool to the Home Office in 1792[1] stated the difficulty:

> For, sir, in all these places are nothing but Methodist and other Meeting Houses, and as the people in the country are in general disposed to go to some place of Worship on Sunday, they go to these because there is no other; and thus the youth of the country are trained up under the instruction of a set of men not only ignorant, but whom I think we have of late too much reason to imagine are inimical to our happy Constitution.

The charge of revolution, however unjust, was to be heard again whenever men wished to blacken the reputation of Methodists; the charge of missionary activity was more justified by events. New industrial towns which had had no parish church had flourishing Methodist Societies and Circuits, and the efforts of the awakened Church did not weaken the hold of the Chapels upon the working classes. Until late in the nineteenth century, Methodism retained that predominantly urban character stamped upon it by the conditions of its rise in the eighteenth century. Rural circuits there were, but it was not until the eighties of the nineteenth century that the great *organised* development of "Village Methodism" came.

The contention that Methodism, after the fashion of

[1] Quoted Hammond, *The Town Labourer*, p. 270.

all great evangelical movements in the Church, flourished best in virgin or fallow soil, is borne out by its fate in Scotland. In spite of several missionary journeys by Wesley, Methodism never flourished north of the Tweed.[1] Presbyterianism had there an unshakable hold upon the people, and the revival in the Scottish Church accomplished there a work analogous to that of Methodism in England. In Ireland, no Protestant revival could hope to win the Irish from their native Catholicism; but in Wales the comparative weakness of Methodism was due to the successful rivalry of Whitefield and his Calvinistic Methodism.

It was in industrial England that the work of Wesley and his colleagues bore most abiding fruit. Both the weakness of the organisation of the Church of England and the methods of the Methodists led to that result. The Societies grew by the personal evangelism of their members amongst those with whom they lived and worked, and, in the crowded cities of the new industrialism, they found scope for such activities. "Wesleyanism and Industrialism were soon to make a new world between Trent and Tweed".[2]

The geographical distribution of the "United Societies" had effect upon their history chiefly because it determined the social strata from which the revival drew its leaders in the period during which Methodism changed into a Nonconformist denomination, and because its industrial environment changed the character of a movement, initiated by an Oxford scholar, but spread by the

[1] There were only 1086 members in Scotland in 1791.
[2] Trevelyan, *History of England*, p. 531.

children of the new industrial society of the nineteenth century. W. J. Warner has traced the occupations of sixty-three of Wesley's preachers and has shown how they were drawn from

a fairly homogeneous group, ranging just below and just above the lower-middle class—that is, skilled artisans, small tradesmen and small farmers. Practically all of the regular preachers, therefore, during this period of more than fifty years [the first generation of Methodism] were drawn from a single social stratum, located between "unskilled labour" and "middle class".[1]

If it be true that this predominance was emphasised by the tendency of the Methodist upper classes to produce candidates for Holy Orders, rather than for the exacting itinerancy—a tendency encouraged by the Wesleys themselves—a glance at the other two categories of Methodist offices tends to confirm the first impression. Aristocrats and professional men, though not absent, have always been relatively scarce in the movement, but wealthy shopkeepers, merchants, and manufacturers have often been Methodist local preachers, and there was not at first any great difference between local and itinerant preachers.[2] Unskilled labourers have also played a prominent part in the history of local preaching.

The class leaders were drawn from roughly the same social grades as the local preachers, and rarely were they recruited from any ranks above the middle class. If it is untrue to say that they composed a democratic institution,

[1] *Op. cit.* p. 250.
[2] Many itinerants continued the pursuit of their original occupations until Wesley forbade the practice in 1768.

in that they were appointed (or their appointments necessarily ratified) by Wesley, they did embody a great equalising tradition, which paid little or no attention to the economic or social position of the men who were judged fit to control the spiritual affairs of the Societies. The equalising tendency might have been less easy had there been more of the upper classes in the United Societies. As it was, it was comparatively easy for middle and working classes—especially when other factors were helping to weld them into a new middle class—to allow their religion to break down the middle wall of partition between them.

What was true of the leaders was true of the people; for, apart from the handful of Anglican clerics at the head of affairs, the leaders were recruited from the Societies, and so those leaders may be taken as fairly representative of the social classes predominating in Methodism. Preaching to the outcasts and to the unevangelised poor, Wesley had attracted many working-class members. The peculiarly Methodist institution of the "Class", with its regular contributions,[1] was in one aspect one of his many attempts to relieve the distress of his working-class followers. The location of the chief Societies in the industrial areas, and the predominance of the "lower-middle" and working classes in the Societies, were both fruits of the same movement, a movement led by a handful of clerics assisted by members of the classes to which they appealed. Methodism was one of the great "People's Movements" in modern history. In a world which was

[1] Members had to pay at least a penny per week "Class Money" unless their poverty prevented them, and then they were granted assistance.

passing away, in which old ideas, manners, and customs were giving place to new,

> He (John Wesley) alone had the key to the hearts of the new England that was growing up in the towns and industrialised villages.[1]

His followers were men and women of those classes which were, in the nineteenth century, to become the powerful "Liberal" classes.

Not only did the geographical and social environment of early Methodism play its part in moulding its character, but so also did the "Time Factor". When John Wesley "launched the Reaction", social and religious life in England may be said to have been quiescent if not stagnant; when he relinquished the helm half a century later, the eighteenth century had been changed by the Industrial Revolution and stirred to its depths by the French Revolution. Walpole's "Let sleeping dogs lie" had given place to the revolutionary slogan "Liberty, Equality, and Fraternity". Lecky and Halévy have suggested that Methodism saved England from a revolution akin to that in France,[2] but Methodism itself did not

[1] J. D. Chambers, *Nottinghamshire in the Eighteenth Century*, p. 328.

[2] Professor Clapham doubts the truth of this contention: but that revolutionary ideas were "abroad" at this time, and that they had a great effect in moulding English political thinking, both in action and reaction, cannot be doubted. Edwards (*op. cit.*), Chapter VI, examines the contentions of both schools, and concludes that "Wesley did not avert a revolution in England, for whether he had lived or not, that would never have happened: but it can legitimately be argued that because of his work and influence the impact of the Revolution was softened, and England was far less disturbed" (p. 96).

escape the effect of ideas which permeated the atmosphere at the close of the century.

Wesley had done his best to keep his Societies clear of
politics and political entanglements. He had been helped
in this by the absence of political interest amongst most
of his followers, and by the positive force of his spiritual
message, with its imperious demand upon the whole life
of men. But when ideas are "in the air", in the way that
the French Revolutionary ideas were, they make their
impress upon minds not primarily concerned with their
effects in one particular sphere. The doctrines of this
new Liberalism entered Methodism almost subcon-
sciously, but they bore fruit with a more than indirect
bearing upon both its nature and its development.
Democratic and Radical ideas, such as were in the minds
and on the lips of multitudes, crept into Methodism, and
made its members regard with critical eyes the paternal
government left by John Wesley. "Natural and Inde-
feasible Rights of Man", "Liberty, Equality, and Fraternity", "Vox Populi Vox Dei", all these catchwords
of the Revolution found their way into eighteenth-
century Methodism. They assumed a theological rather
than a political significance, and it was not hard for men
of Radical temper to find Biblical support for their creed.
Men who had drunk of the wine of revolutionary teaching
often read their Bibles in a new light. Liberty, Equality,
and Fraternity were exalted into a new divinely sanc-
tioned trinity of ultimate values. They were held to be
of equal worth, and they tended to replace the old belief
in natural human depravity by a doctrine of the divine
right of the free people. Rousseau was the prophet of the

new age. His idealised picture of the "noble savage" appealed to all classes. In the name of their real nature, men might demand to govern their own affairs, and, once men were given the freedom to do this, there would be established the ideal state upon earth. It was a theory calculated to infuse a generous enthusiasm into men newly awakening to the possibilities of political activity.

Wesley's emphasis had been different. Both men had been individualists, but, whilst Rousseau had looked to an ideal state, in which men might find full scope for their activities, Wesley had concentrated upon the individual's conversion. Wesley had not felt it necessary to direct the energies of his converts towards the reforming of the State; he had left that to the gradual work of the men directly concerned in government. Rousseau's work was essentially political; Wesley's essentially religious. Wesley's followers found themselves influenced by both sets of ideas, and their Wesleyan theology became modified by the doctrine of "Natural Rights" which was propagated by Rousseau and his disciples.

That ideas of the natural rights of man grew implicitly before they were given explicit utterance may have retarded the actual revolution they worked, but that revolution nevertheless took place. The ideas of the French Revolution were amongst the first which began the process of breaking up the Wesleyan Reaction, for they made men question the right of any form of government "for" rather than "by" the people. Dissenters who had become Methodists gave the Radical element strength, and their tradition made them chary of, if not hostile to, Wesley's paternalism.

64

The conflict between the forces of the " Reaction " and the forces of Liberalism was a protracted one, but the trial of strength was averted during Wesley's lifetime, by the love and reverence with which, amongst his followers, he was universally regarded. As soon as he was dead, the struggle which was to change the nature of "Wesleyan" Methodism began. Liberalism never won a complete victory, but it so entered into the life of nineteenth-century Methodism that the term "Wesleyan Reaction " is now of interest from an antiquarian rather than from a practical standpoint. At first, the reformers made little headway, but it was not mere coincidence that connected in time the first internal disturbances within Methodism with the era of the French Revolution. When revolution was infectious, Methodism could not escape; but the results were mild, and convalescence rapid.

The death of John Wesley in 1791 removed the man who had acted as the pivot of Methodist organisation. The history of the years immediately following his removal from the sphere he had always dominated supplies an eloquent comment upon his *Apology* of 1766. If the real strength of military command lies in its unity and concentration at one point, the same had been true of Methodism; but, now that the commander-in-chief was dead, there was no one to take his place. When Wesley was dying, his travelling companion, Joseph Bradford, sent out to the Societies the simple message, "Pray, Pray, Pray ", and it was Methodism, rather than Wesley, that needed the prayers. A man who, by the force of his own personality, had ruled his brethren, who had made the decisions of his Church according to circumstances

65

and the light of his conscience for fifty years, who had created the machinery through which he had worked, who had been loved and honoured by those he had led, and who had had no other to share his responsibility with him, was a man whose loss could not but entail for his movement difficulties of a most far-reaching kind. The very life of Methodism depended upon the solution of those difficulties, and, in the six troubled years which followed Wesley's death, decisive steps were taken.

There had been discontent in Methodism before 1791, and especially during the last decade of Wesley's life, but love for an old man, and perhaps knowledge that a man over eighty could not live much longer, had postponed the struggle and kept it under ground.[1] As soon as he was dead the strife began, and it did not die down until the acceptance of an important constitutional change and the establishment of a new Methodist Connexion had radically modified the Methodism of John Wesley, and had begun that "Liberalising" movement which was in some ways the most remarkable feature of the nineteenth-century break-up of the Wesleyan Reaction. It is the purpose of this essay to trace the connexion between these two aspects of Methodist history—the break-up of the Reaction and the contemporary genesis of the Methodist Liberal.

Of the necessary difficulties arising from the death of Wesley the most obvious, and the most pressing, was the

---

[1] See the declaration to this effect at the beginning of the pamphlet written by (or for) the Nottingham trustees in 1797 and entitled *A brief statement of the dispute and cause of division amongst Methodists at Nottingham, Sheffield, Leeds, Manchester, etc.*

question of his successor. It was on this point that feeling in the Church ran most high. In 1766 Wesley had claimed that the people would submit to him alone, and his death revealed that the same was true of his preachers. By 1784 he had realised that there was no one man amongst his coadjutors capable of taking his place, and so he had vested supreme power in the Conference: but he had taken the precaution of asking the " Legal Hundred" for a promise that they would not abuse their power in their relations with their brother-ministers. He had done this because of criticisms from men, not mentioned in the Deed Poll, who were jealous of the influence of certain of the old man's advisers. Wesley hoped, however, that the members of Conference would exercise the authority committed to them in as considerate a way as he had done himself.

To those who were left, the tyranny of Conference seemed a different thing from the benevolent despotism of the " Father " of Methodism,[1] and meetings were held and memorials sent round in every part of the Connexion. Mather and Dr Coke, who had both been ordained by Wesley as Superintendents,[2] were suspected of a design to impose an episcopal form of government upon Methodism. The scheme was however brought to naught by the united opposition of the rest of the Church, and, as a safeguard, it was resolved at the first Conference after Wesley's death that the President and Secretary should

[1] The Nottingham Trustees' pamphlet attacked "this self-elected and self-created body", i.e. Conference.
[2] In these ordinations Wesley was careful not to use the term "Bishop".

only hold office for one Conference at a time.[1] The equality of the preachers was vindicated, and the District Meetings were to exercise authority in the intervals between Conferences. The question of the relations between Conference, District Meetings, Circuits, and Societies, and their corresponding rights, remained to be decided.

Another great unsolved problem was that of the relations between the ministry and the laity. Conference and the District Meetings were exclusively ministerial bodies, but in the conduct of Circuit and Society business, the laity played a much more prominent part. Most of the property of the Church was vested in trustees, who, not unnaturally, were unlikely to acquiesce in their lack of governing power. Wesley had realised the danger when he was persuaded by his friends to take the affairs of the "New Room" at Bristol into his own hands in 1739:

Many reasons they gave for this; but one was enough, viz., "That such feoffees always would have it in their power to control me; and if I preached not as they liked, to turn me out of the room I had built". I accordingly yielded to their advice; and calling all the feoffees together, cancelled (no man opposing) the instrument made before, and took the whole management into my own hands.[2]

But the spread of Methodist Chapels throughout the

[1] "The President of the Wesleyan Methodist Conference is annually chosen by a silent ballot of the ministers without nomination or speeches—a method of election that is, we believe, without parallel save for the Papal chair. He must, of course, be a minister. Theoretically he is 'President' only of Conference, and with the Conference his powers originally lapsed. But practice has long since outgrown the restrictions imposed by early jealousy of any successor to Wesley's autocracy." H. B. Workman, *Methodism* (Cambridge Manuals), p. 124 n.   [2] *Journal*, May 12th, 1739.

country prevented Wesley's following the precedent he had hoped to establish in his relations to his trust property. If chapels were to be built and financed, and both the growth of the movement and the hostility of the clergy made building a necessity, lay trustees would have to be used. During Wesley's lifetime they played their part without causing trouble, but when he died, they formed a powerful section of the Church to whom malcontents might appeal for help against the clerical dominance of Conference. Wesley had left unsolved the question of the relations between the ministry and the laity, because, not realising how far he had gone towards founding a new Church, he had not seen its imminence; when it came up for discussion during the six troubled years that followed 1791, it was the trustees, not the local preachers and class leaders, who were chiefly involved.

The third great problem left at Wesley's death was that of the relations between Methodism and the Church of England. What position was Methodism to take in English religious life? Were the "United Societies" to remain, as Wesley seems to have hoped, means of quickening the religious life of the national Church? Were they, alternatively, to break with their mother church and to constitute themselves a new denomination, more or less dissenting? By forbidding his preachers to administer the sacraments, and by holding Methodist services outside the normal hours for Church worship, Wesley had tried to prevent a breach he did not wish. With his death passed also the clerical "General Staff" which had been one of his strongest supports, and Methodism was left to settle its position without the guidance of most of those who had resisted the departure of the movement from its Anglican origins.

The majority of Methodists, both clerical and lay, did not wish to break with the Church in which they had been baptized and reared, but circumstances were often too much for them. More than one Methodist preacher had to avail himself of the protection of the Toleration Act by obtaining a Dissenting Minister's licence. Intolerant clergy refused to admit Methodist parishioners to the benefits of Church life, and the followers of the man who had brought into English life afresh the practice of constant communion were denied access to it. It was an insupportable position, and, as Wesley was faced with the problem of separation when he contemplated "field preaching" and the ordination of his Superintendents, so Methodism was faced with the same problem concerning communion and worship during Church hours.

Personal jealousies amongst the preachers confused the issue, but all the circular letters and pamphlets written at this time were focused on these three problems. None admitted of easy solution. The first was reasonably settled by vindicating the equality of the preachers by the provisions of the Conference of 1791;[1] the second was a latent difficulty throughout the period covered by this essay; the third demanded immediate attention and produced important modifications and reforms. The Plan of Pacification in 1795[2] attempted to

[1] See above, pp. 67–8, and the *Minutes for the Conference of* 1791.
[2] See Peirce, pp. 778–81, for a copy of this document. Part I is "Concerning the Lord's Supper, Baptism, etc.".

solve the difficulty. In no Methodist Society might the sacraments be administered without the express sanction of Conference, but, where they had previously been administered without trouble arising, or where a clear majority of trustees, stewards, and leaders desired such facilities, that sanction might be given. The form to be used was safeguarded by definite regulations, and in no case were the sacraments to be administered in Methodist Chapels on days when the Church of England was holding such services. A special vote was necessary before they might be held during Church hours.

The Plan of Pacification was the culmination of a series of compromises which Conference had had to make, and, if it succeeded in pacifying the great majority of Methodists, as it undoubtedly did, it also served to mark the definite separation of Methodism from the Church of England. From 1795 Methodism must be regarded as a Church, not simply as a Connexion composed of "United Societies". The Plan of Pacification was one of Methodism's great steps in its long and unforeseen gravitation towards Dissent.

There were certain of the preachers who were dissatisfied with the provisions of the Plan of Pacification, and who considered that the taking of a Dissenting licence involved acceptance of a Dissenting position. They had little patience with the middle course pursued by Conference, and, could they have had their way, would have carried to their logical conclusion all the equalising tendencies in Methodism. They were apt to be doctrinaire, to appeal to general principles, and to press their side of the case in point as far as it would go.

They were the men most affected by the French Revolution; and they became the leaders of the "Radical party" in Methodism. In Church government they wanted democracy, equality among the preachers, and the admission of the laity to all Church courts; in the Church at large, they desired openly to avow the Dissenting position that the hostility of the Church of England had made them take up in practice; in politics their sympathies were with those Whigs who favoured Parliamentary Reform.[1]

Of these men, the articulate leader and archetype was Alexander Kilham,[2] the first great "Liberal Methodist". He was an ardent and zealous young man whose early death[3] was the result of his being worn out by evangelism and agitation combined. Although he led the discontented minority and was the chief mover in the establishment of the Methodist New Connexion, he was faithful to Methodist tradition in his activity as a preacher. His faults were the faults of his nature: tactlessness, failure to see any value in compromise, and a too logical adherence to his principles. He foreshadowed that union of eighteenth-century Methodist fervour with nineteenth-century Nonconformist "principle" which marked the Methodist Liberal. His sincerity and disinterestedness are not open to question, but that he should have been misunderstood by his brethren was almost inevitable. He was too much a doctrinaire to work quietly amidst the anomalies of the Methodism left by Wesley.

[1] See Blackwell's *Life of Kilham*, pp. 340–1.
[2] See Blackwell's *Life of Kilham* for an account and an appreciation.
[3] He was only 36 when he died.

Kilham is important, both as an individual—he was one of the most interesting men in Methodist history—and as a leader of that section of the Connexion which was dissatisfied with Methodism's slow rate of progress towards Dissent. His spirit was antagonistic to many of the features of Wesley's "Reaction", and it fitted him to become the first leader of the movement away from it. Alexander Kilham was the "morning star" of Liberal Methodism, before whose light the "Wesleyan Reaction" waned.

Kilham had been one of the men who had anticipated changes after the death of Wesley, and who was jealous for the equality of the preachers and the rights of the laity. He hoped that Methodism would become free to develop, as he believed it ought to develop, into a great Dissenting Church.[1] He was soon drawn into the pamphlet war that broke out in 1791, and his first efforts were made in reply to the "Church Methodists'" restriction of the sacraments to parish churches.[2] For the next seven years his pen was scarcely ever idle. Letters, pamphlets, his magazine *The Methodist Monitor*, all these he produced untiringly. It was little wonder that this labour, superimposed upon the rigorous life of a Methodist itinerant, brought about his premature death in 1798.

Although, unlike most Englishmen, Kilham was enamoured of the logic of first principles, he began his agitation in a typically English way, by attacking specific

[1] That Wesley himself was not unaware of this possibility is borne out by his remarks on the "Presbyterian Meeting House" Chapel at Glasgow in May 1788—*Journal*, May 16th, 1788.
[2] See his reply to the letter of the Trustees of Hull, Blackwell, pp. 128–34.

abuses in the life of the Church. Financial administration had produced scandals; Kilham pressed for the presentation of public accounts;[1] people who had been taught to celebrate as often as possible were denied access to the sacrament;[2] he flung himself against the " Church party " which was patently the party of restriction; the laity, and especially the trustees, felt themselves injured by their lack of power; Kilham's pen was recruited in their service. In all these matters he was tilting at real difficulties. Had the grievances been redressed in time, it is possible that such a zealous preacher might have found sufficient outlet for his energies in the work of the itinerancy. As it happened, he was led further and further into the sphere of ecclesiastical controversy; and from abortive efforts to gain reform he was driven to a much more serious advocacy of revolt. The history of the New Connexion controversy is akin to that of many another English revolutionary movement—unsatisfied attempts to gain reform followed by a general attack upon the foundations of the system needing reform.

Some of the older preachers resented the criticisms of this " young man " Kilham, and the controversialists soon had recourse to the weapons of personal abuse. Both sides began to indulge in invective: but, much more important, Kilham struck the first blows against the system of the " Reaction ". The doctrinaire elements in his character came into play as he prepared to question the

---

[1] See *The Methodist Monitor*, in which he carried on the agitation.
[2] See *An Earnest Address by Paul and Silas* and also *The Progress of Liberty*, both written by Kilham in 1795.

fundamental assumptions and general usefulness of a system he had at first only sought to reform. John Wesley had been a practical man, more concerned with the actual efficiency of the machinery he used than with its theoretic justification; Alexander Kilham had a passion for logical consistency that made him a thoroughgoing Radical, and an unflinching opponent of anything savouring of autocracy in either Church or State. In the controversy which led up to the establishment of a new Methodist Connexion in 1797, the influence of French Revolutionary ideas upon Kilham's thought was marked. It was this especially which justified the description of his movement as the first "Liberal" movement in Methodism.

The Conference of 1791 had resolved "to follow Mr Wesley's plan", but subsequent events showed how many contradictory interpretations of that plan could be given, and used to bolster the case of either side. Coke and Mather interpreted it one way; Kilham appealed to it to sanction his opposition to their ambitions. Seizing on all the precedents set by Wesley in his innovations, Kilham maintained that, if Methodism were to be true to its real spirit—and he appealed to the spirit rather than to the letter of Wesley's work[1]—it must develop those elements of latent democracy that he read in its constitution. He realised the strength of Wesley's paternal control over the infant Societies, but he felt that, in the system of Conference, Leaders' Meetings, and bodies of trustees, were seeds of a democratic representative system, seeds which would, in the full-grown Societies,

[1] See *An Earnest Address by Paul and Silas* (1795), pp. 3–6.

bear abundant fruit. It was for the cultivation of this fruit that he was working.

Pastoral supremacy had been a necessary stage in the development of the infant Church, and John Wesley's autocracy had been indispensable, but these, according to Kilham, were but the leading strings of ecclesiastical childhood.[1] Now that Methodism had grown up, it ought to be treated as responsible. In this case, argued Kilham, Methodism was ready for more democratic government, because only so, in any full-grown society, could its members fulfil their personalities, or could that Society be satisfactorily governed. The death of Wesley had marked the end of the period of "probation", and had made possible this free and rational development of the democracy inherent in the Church from its beginning.

This Plan being adopted, made us a pure republic...our emulation was, *to be equal—to be brethren in Christ Jesus.*[2]

Not only were the ministers to be equal, but the lay trustees and leaders were to exercise far greater authority in Society and Circuit affairs than had been customary in most of the Circuits under John Wesley's supervision. Kilham wanted lay representation in Conference and District Meetings, and seems to have been an admirer of Congregational Church polity, except in so far as it would have undermined the itinerancy, which he, as much as anyone, was anxious to conserve. All these reforms in Church government he believed to be in the spirit of "Mr Wesley's plan", and, with his Liberal ideas

[1] See *Outlines of a Constitution*, p. 22.
[2] *An Earnest Address by Paul and Silas*, p. 13.

about infant Societies and their "coming of age", he was more concerned to discover the spirit of that plan than to observe its literal provisions.

It was this appeal to the spirit of John Wesley which gave Kilham's arguments point. Revolutionaries usually begin by avowing that their proposals are consonant with hallowed tradition, and yet, because their vision is warped by preconceived ideas, they are rarely correct. Kilham's historical sense had been twisted by the French Revolution's ideas of Liberty, Equality, and Fraternity, its plea for the representation of the people, and all those Liberal principles which would appeal so strongly to an ardent young Methodist preacher, anxious to redress the grievances of his brethren. He overlooked the essentially autocratic character of Methodist organisation, and saw only the semblance of democratic institutions. He was perhaps the first Methodist to see in the system democratic elements which had formed no part of Wesley's intention. That he was in a minority in holding this view is relatively unimportant, because his real significance lies in the way he foreshadowed later developments. His perhaps distorted view of John Wesley's work was to become the accepted belief of great bodies of Methodists in the next century. It was an unhistoric view; but it was a prophetic one. John Wesley would have rejected it; the Liberal Methodists of the nineteenth century set it amongst their first principles, and gave to it a reality it had not possessed in the first years of the movement.

Kilham's pamphlets furnish interesting examples of this Radical reasoning. *The Methodist Monitor*, of which he published two volumes, was a religious magazine composed of religious news, sermons, controversial articles in which he answered his opponents with fearless reasonableness, and, perhaps most interesting of all, reprints of works on Church government by men like Watts and other Independents, side by side with his own reprinted pamphlets. The *Monitor* was his chief vehicle of agitation, but he also wrote and dispersed widely[1] several pamphlets in which he propounded his theories. The *Earnest Appeal of Paul and Silas*, the *Progress of Liberty* and the *Outlines of a Constitution*, all written in 1795, and other pamphlets written both before and after that date, were meant to convince his fellow-Methodists of the Wesleyan and scriptural character of his proposals. They were, moreover, intended to show that his proposals were more consistent with the "natural order of society" than were the arguments of his opponents. He appealed, not only to John Wesley and to the Bible, but also to the privileges of men "as Christians and as Britons".[2] In the *Outlines of a Constitution*[3] he maintained that Methodist doctrines ought to be examined to see which were scriptural, and that all unscriptural elements should be purged; yet, almost immediately afterwards, he was to be found objecting to the ministerial appointments of class leaders without the people's consent, as an attack upon the rights of the people.[4] Then follows his great Liberal assertion:

[1] These pamphlets were written and sent anonymously for fear that, if the author's name were known, his works would be returned unread and he would be ruined by the cost of postage, which was, in the days before Rowland Hill, very considerable—and not prepaid. Had the cost of postage and distribution been added to the cost of publication, there might soon have been an end to all pamphlet wars amongst Methodist ministers.

[2] *The Progress of Liberty*, p. 17. [3] P. 24. [4] *Ibid.* p. 26.

"Ever considering that the cool dispassionate voice of the people is the voice of God."[1] Perhaps no quotation could so succinctly reveal the influence of the French Revolution on Kilham's thought, or show how far he had moved from the position of Wesley's *Apology* of 1766. Kilham's method of argument by the ascription of Biblical authority to general Rights of Man reads strangely like the arguments of "theological Free Traders" and Nonconformist Liberals of the nineteenth century.

Kilham could have had little idea how far French Revolutionary ideas had affected his interpretation of the Bible, when, after asserting the Pauline doctrine that we should "call no man master save Christ", he drew the conclusion that

We all have an equal right to vote in these matters as we are all redeemed by Christ, and have each a soul to save, equally precious in the sight of God....[2]

But whether he knew it or not, such doctrine was as a battle cry to the middle classes just awakening to a political consciousness. Kilham's own following was small, but he was as the first stone that starts an avalanche. The Liberal Methodists eagerly accepted these doctrines of his, and found in them a scriptural warrant for their democratic attack on privilege, alike in Church and State. Their first battles were often fought out in church meetings, protesting against the autocracy of the preacher; but, with their emphasis upon the sufficiency of the Bible as a rule of life and their "Liberal"[3] interpretation of it, they carried those same struggles against authority

[1] *Ibid.* p. 34. [2] *Ibid.* p. 36.
[3] "Liberal" is used here in a political, not a theological sense.

into the sphere of national politics. They were citizens with rights in the British State, but, in civic as in religious matters, they paid homage to the infallibility of the Bible. All the literature of this controversy, and of the movement under consideration in this essay, furnishes examples of this all-important fact, that the movement began, and remained, essentially a religious one. Both sides accepted the sovereignty of the Bible; it was the interpretation accepted by either side that determined its alignment on matters both ecclesiastical and political.

The agitation which followed upon Wesley's death reached a climax in 1796 when the arch-malcontent Kilham was tried by Conference.[1] As he refused to withdraw objectionable references to Methodist polity in his writings, he was expelled. That he was misjudged and that justice was hardly given him in his trial is true, but there are things to be said in extenuation even of the blundering of Conference. They cannot be fully exonerated from the charge of lack of sympathy, but Kilham's tactless idealism was exasperating. With revolution and war about them, with the mobs so easily stirred up against "Jacobins", with their own problems of Church government to solve, and with the saddle of Wesley empty, they were bewildered, and as men without a leader. They had granted substantial concessions to the spirit of reform, but the Plan of Pacification marked the limit of those concessions, and it was true that the majority, even amongst those Methodists who cared about

[1] For an account of the proceedings at this interesting trial see Blackwell, Chapter VII, or the account which Kilham himself published.

such matters, had been satisfied. Those who were still
dissatisfied, and who felt with Kilham that the Plan of
1795 showed how far was Methodism "from that liberty
of conscience which was their privilege as Christians
and Britons",[1] could no longer be accommodated in a
Connexion in which sovereign power lay with a clerical
Conference.

In 1797 William Thom[2] and two other preachers re-
signed, and, in collaboration with Alexander Kilham,
formed a new Methodist Connexion. Sympathisers
amongst the laity, many of them local preachers and
trustees, joined them, and the infant Church, the first
of the "Free" Methodist Churches, began with about
5000 members, drawn chiefly from growing industrial
Circuits. The first Conference of the Methodist New
Connexion was held at Leeds in 1797, and the first entry
in its Minutes reads:

Q. 1. What places, seeking a redress of grievances, in the
connexion, are desirous of supporting a new itinerancy, since
that redress cannot be had?

A. A Part of the Sheffield Society and Circuit. Also of
Nottingham, Banbury, Burslem, Macclesfield, Chester,
Liverpool, Wigan, Bolton, Blackburn, Manchester, Oldham,
Huddersfield, Leeds, Epworth, Otley, Ripon, Newcastle,
Alnwick &c. and several places in those as well as in other
circuits.[3]

[1] *The Progress of Liberty*, p. 17.
[2] Thom, who had been one of Wesley's Dissenting helpers, had
been nominated by him into "The Hundred".
[3] The New Connexion followed Wesley's precedent in recording
the Minutes of Conference in the form of question and answer.
The title-page of the copy of *M.N.C.* Minutes for 1797 in the Hobill
Collection has been mutilated by "apposite" emendations by a
contemporary enemy of the young Church.

A further question showed that there had been ten travelling preachers, but that two had left the new itinerancy. It was suggested that vacancies should be filled by suitable local preachers being called out, "by the choice of the people".

Considering the character of many of these places and the composition of their Societies, the fact that they were the birth-places of a new and more liberal Methodism need cause little surprise. It was evident, from the proceedings of this first Conference of the New Connexion, that the democratic leaven had been, and was, at work amongst the classes most susceptible to its activity. The issue had been joined over questions of Church government, "Rights of Man", and democratic principles. Such a movement was bound to be small, for it could only appeal to men to whom such ideas had meaning and significance, and it was natural that its chief strength should be found in the great industrial centres of the north and midlands. The Wesleyan Methodists spoke more truly than the dissentients would admit when, in their address to their Irish brethren, they said:

We shall lose all the turbulent disturbers of our Zion—all who have embraced the sentiments of Paine, and place a great part of their religion in contending for (what they call) liberty.[1]

The Methodist New Connexion might justifiably resent comparison with an infidel, but its members dreamed in religion the same dream as Paine in politics. When their religion and politics were wedded, they produced the

[1] Quoted Blackwell, p. 339.

Liberalism which almost invariably was the political counterpart of "Free Methodism". Benson, Mather, and Pawson, had roused Kilham's resentment when they had said:

There is little likelihood of his drawing off any, but those whose views accord with his own in politics as well as religion...

but there was to grow up a generation which would not echo Kilham's retort:

What has our plan to do with politics?[1]

The prophetic nature of the taunt could not have been suspected by either party in the controversy.

The nature of the new Church may perhaps best be realised in an examination of the answers it offered to the three questions left unsolved at the death of Wesley. The first question, that of the leadership of the Church and the danger of oligarchic tyranny in Conference, was settled, as in Wesleyan Methodism, by the annual election of the officers of Conference. (Thom and Kilham were respectively elected President and Secretary in 1797.) On the other hand, Thom, who was an Aberdonian by birth, and Kilham, who had "travelled" there, had both been influenced by Presbyterian polity. They modified the centralisation of Wesleyan Methodism in accordance with Presbyterian models. The last word still remained with Conference, but Districts, Circuits, and Societies were all given wider powers of jurisdiction and decision. Congregationalism would have destroyed the itinerancy,[2] and was too extreme to serve as a model for

[1] *The Methodist Monitor*, p. 231.
[2] See *Outlines of a Constitution*, p. 32.

a Methodist Connexion, but there was sufficient similarity between Presbyterianism and Methodism for the reformers to find in it a model for a democratic Connexionalism.

By its very nature the reform movement was chiefly concerned with the second problem, that of the relations between the ministry and the laity. Here these reformers were master builders, and they were responsible for initiating that modification of the Reaction which has, by its acceptance in the new Methodist Church, come to affect the whole of Methodism, namely, the equal representation of the ministry and the laity in Conference, and the vindication of laymen's rights to be represented in all Church courts.[1] It was here that the New Connexion made its greatest contribution, alike to the democratic development of Methodism, and to the modification of the Reaction. New Connexion Methodists had been prepared to suffer denominational exile for this principle; it became the corner-stone of their ecclesiastical edifice. The trustees had tried to set up a "lay house of Conference" by holding meetings of lay delegates in the same town and at the same time as the clerical Conference was sitting; but the old Conference had refused to recognise the validity of such meetings.[2] Consequently these laymen were more ready than ever to sit side by side with their ministers in the new Church's Conference. In this

[1] By the provisions of the new Methodist Union Act (which came into force in September 1932) the "Legal Hundred" is abolished, but the Wesleyan "Pastoral Session" remains. Otherwise there is equal clerical and lay representation.

[2] This was one of the grievances catalogued by the Nottingham Trustees in their *Brief Statement* of 1797, p. 5. (See above, p. 66 n.)

way potential clashes were avoided and co-operation fostered. The provisions of its constitution, allowing laymen to find redress of grievances without resort to violent measures, preserved the New Connexion from the discord which disgraced nineteenth-century Wesleyan Methodism. The young Church was not torn in the nineteenth century by the struggles of laymen against ministerial autocracy, but it took other Methodist Connexions generations to learn the lesson read to them by these seemingly premature revolutionaries.

The New Connexion Methodists' attitude to the last of the three great problems eased their development towards political Liberalism, because it ranked them definitely with the Dissenters. Kilham had been compelled by persecution to take out a Dissenting minister's licence under the provisions of the Toleration Act, and, with his usual logic, he had decided that henceforth he must accept the reality of his Nonconformist position. He regarded himself as a Dissenter in fact as well as in theory, and he had therefore little patience with the great efforts made by the "Church Methodists" to preserve the link between Methodism and the Church of England. The practical hardship of the loss of communion services, allied to theories of natural rights, had made Kilham an uncompromising advocate of Methodist sacraments. Methodist Dissenters supported him, and, when the New Connexion was established, its preachers claimed the full right of administering Baptism and the Lord's Supper in their own chapels and during Church service hours. Their nicknames in Huddersfield—"Sacramentarians" and "Tom Paine Methodists"—were neither of them misnomers. Both pointed to elements essential to the thought and practice of Kilham and his movement. As many of the New Connexion Methodists owed their spiritual allegiance to the Dissenting Churches, they did not feel a breach with the national Church to be any hardship, and, as the New Connexion broke from its Wesleyan origins and ranged itself alongside the old Nonconformist Churches, it put itself under the influence of the old Whig-Dissenting alliance—a circumstance which played no unimportant part in rearing its nascent Liberalism.

The influence of this factor was particularly increased because these ecclesiastically-minded malcontents were only beginning to have any political consciousness, and their minds were plastic in the fateful generation before 1832. It is not difficult to see which side would be taken in questions affecting the franchise by men who believed that men, as rational and normal beings, have a natural right to property, that the end of government is the welfare of the governed, that, although there is no infallible means of ensuring this, only by democracy can the needs of the governed be directly made known, that the representative principle must apply to the highest courts, and that these principles are to apply alike to civil and religious matters.[1] In religion they drew the conclusion that Church members had the right to be represented in Church government, that ministers were entitled to respect, but as they were liable to err, they must have the assistance and counsel of their Church members, and

[1] See *An Exposition of the Principles of Church Government adopted by the Methodist New Connexion*, being an address by the Rev. T. Allin, given at Sheffield in 1833. Note the date and the opinions expressed.

86

that this association of Church members and "Pastors" was a New Testament doctrine,

The authority of the ministry therefore is only such as harmonizes with the right of judgement in the people expressed and exercised as circumstances may require.[1]

because the right of judgment was vested in the people by the New Testament. When these were their conclusions as to Church government, it is not hard to see what would be their usual attitude to political questions, and New Connexion biographies bear out the contention here maintained. Both ecclesiastically and politically New Connexion Methodists could (and did)[2] claim to be "Liberal Methodists".

[1] *Ibid.* p. 7.
[2] See the controversy between Dr Watts and the Editor in *The Wesleyan Methodist Magazine* for 1877.

CHAPTER IV

RÉVIVALS AND REACTION:
METHODISM FROM 1797 TO 1827

The first quarter of the nineteenth century was deeply influenced by great movements. Socially and economically, it was a period of change and industrialisation; politically, it was moulded by the French Revolution, its ideas, its results, its hopes and its fears; culturally and artistically, Romanticism swept the field; religiously, in England at least, the Evangelical Movement had its period of greatest activity and influence. In every sphere of life there were great causes claiming men's allegiance; in every sphere of life there were great forces at work reshaping men's thought and action. In a generation the eighteenth century died and the nineteenth was born. The factory system had superseded the old domestic crafts; wealth was passing from the landowners to the new industrial capitalists of the north; the old Whiggism and Toryism, the Venetian oligarchies and aristocratic patronage systems, perished in the period of revolution and war, and, in spite of Eldons and Wellingtons, the way was opening for Gladstones and Disraelis, and their new popular parties; in literature, the poise of the eighteenth century was disturbed by the torrent of new thought and vigorous feeling which flowed from the pens of men like Wordsworth and Coleridge, Byron and Shelley; in religion, the trumpet of the Evangelical Revival

88

was awakening the Church, which, in the eighteenth century, had "slept and rotted in peace".

But, if Wordsworth could sing:

> Bliss was it in that dawn to be alive,
> And to be young was very heaven,

there were many in whose hearts there was no responsive echo. The Industrial Revolution, the war with its blockades and its aftermath, incompetent government, and a lack of sympathy and experience in dealing with the problems of a new age, all swelled the general hardship and discontent which depressed the lower-middle and working classes. For them transition brought little of the inspiration which fired intellectuals, but much drab hardship and suffering. Conditions in the growing towns of the north need no description here, but the contention that the preaching of Heaven gained intensity from the circumstances under which men lived has its quota of truth.

The French Revolution caused fear and uncertainty as much as inspiration. Not only were the "Old Tories"[1] led into repression and reaction, but ordinary men and women, scared by the atrocities of the Revolution and the ambitions of Napoleon, recoiled from doctrines so inflammatory. Tom Paine and Cobbett might speak for masses of their fellow-countrymen, but, to thousands of the people now being affected by the Evangelical Revival, their dogmas (and especially their attacks on religion) were anathema. It was a period when vision and reaction, inspiration and timidity, were strangely mingled, a period

[1] See Dicey, *Law and Public Opinion in England in the Nineteenth Century*, Chapter v.

in which the old gods had perished and "the new hierarchy was not yet established".

The unrest and uncertainty of contemporary thought and life contributed to the triumph of the Evangelical Movement. It had been one of the great factors in breaking up the cultivated self-satisfaction of the eighteenth century, and its own seeds sprang to life in the soil it had ploughed. The time of repose and decay came to an end for both Anglicans and Nonconformists. They had hated the enthusiasm of the Methodists, but the Methodists' sincerity and their success had shamed the older denominations into newness of life and vigour. The Evangelical party in the Church of England came to birth; whilst the Nonconformist Churches, of which so many had lapsed into Unitarianism,[1] were given a new lease of Evangelical life. Wesley had drawn his followers from all types of Christians; but his movement strengthened the numbers as well as the spirit of the old Churches.

Halévy[2] has traced the way the Establishment and the three "Old Denominations" reacted to the new spirit abroad in religion. He has shown how the Church awoke to the abuses which had helped to cripple it in the eighteenth century, and how it strove to remedy some of them.[3] But Evangelicalism did more than reform ecclesiastical abuses. Wesley was driven out of the Church of England, but many of his closest fellow-workers, men such as Venn and Grimshaw, remained in that Church. Their example served to inspire the new party, which,

[1] Most of the "Old Meeting Houses" are lapsed Presbyterian.
[2] In his *History of the English People in* 1815, Book III, Chapter I.
[3] Pp. 384–9.

through Simeon and others, gave to Anglicanism a re-newed zeal. Laymen too, such as Wilberforce and Ash-ley, and the Clapham sect, wielded immense influence. "The Saints" were ready to work with all sorts of Christians, but they were chiefly members of the National Church, and in that Church they accomplished a great work of revival.

In the older Dissenting Churches Methodist influence did its work even more quickly, but less obtrusively. The Dissenters were generally middle-class people, and they came into personal contact with the members of the new sect. Methodist dissensions brought new Methodist churches to take their places beside the "Old Denomina-tions", and, in their everyday lives, middle-class and working-class Nonconformists were continually coming into contact with the Methodists who, socially if not ecclesiastically, were akin to Dissenters rather than to Anglicans. If Nonconformity caught Evangelicalism by contagion and Anglicanism caught it by infection, the result in either case was similar. It has been confidently held that Dissent was saved by the rise of Methodism; the new movement certainly quickened the old bodies' life, whilst, in spite of its protests, Methodism itself was to become the greatest of the Nonconformist Churches.

That Evangelicalism made such an appeal at such a time is not surprising when it is remembered that, in an age of new ideas, new conditions, bewilderment and awakening, its preachers spoke of old truths with the authority of a vivid experience. To men intellectually stale, as were many contemporary divines, to men emo-tionally and spiritually starved, to men for whom life was too much, to those who knew not where certainty might be found, and to masses (especially in the new towns) to whom the Gospel had never been preached, came a message of present deliverance and hope, proclaimed by earnest and zealous men, whose lives of self-sacrifice were often practical demonstrations of the reality of their call. To read side by side the social history of England and the *Lives of the Methodist Preachers*, or John Wesley's *Journal*, is to discover one reason for the spread of the Evangelical Revival.

The opening of the era of "Social Reform" is perhaps the most obvious result of the spiritual awakening of this period. The Clapham sect furnished the Parliamentary spearhead of the movement for the Abolition of Slavery, and, in the nation at large, Evangelicals, Methodists,[1] and Baptists lent enthusiastic support. What Clarkson and Wilberforce and their friends did for the negro slaves, other Evangelicals, led by Oastler, Sadler and Shaftesbury, though unfortunately more slowly, did for the victims of the new industrial régime. The Evangelical Revival was, in fact, marked by great philanthropic energy, exemplified not only by Wesley's experiments in social relief[2] and the Parliamentary activities of the benevolent Tories, but by a wide extension of religious and philanthropic work intended to ameliorate hardships, where they were apparent, and where quickened con-

[1] 229,426 out of 352,404 signatures to a Nonconformist petition in favour of Emancipation were those of Methodists. See Telford, *A Sect that moved the World*, on this and on the Clapham sect and its part in the social reform movements of the period, p. 155.

[2] See especially Edwards, *John Wesley and the Eighteenth Century*, on the nature and scope of these experiments.

sciences perceived them. The benevolence may have been individualist, empiric, and inadequate, but there were sincere attempts to alleviate distress, and to give expression to practical Christianity. This developing sense of social responsibility, of which the Nonconformist conscience to some extent was both a manifestation and a constituent part, was to be a considerable factor in the formation of the Victorian Liberal party.

It is by no means surprising that this aspect of the Evangelical Revival has received much attention from historians, both favourable, like Halévy, and unsympathetic, like the Hammonds. It is in matters of social activity that Churches come most within the view of the world and where, as factors moulding the life of the nation, they can most clearly be seen by social and economic historians. Most modern historians of this period have regarded Evangelicalism as one of the great tributary streams swelling the nineteenth-century humanitarian flood. They have examined the part played by Evangelicals (both Methodists and Anglicans) in the movements towards better conditions, and they have tried to estimate the adequacy of that work and of the social theory it expressed.[1] Following the lead of Max Weber and R. H. Tawney,[2] they have looked at religion from a social-economic point of view. They have estimated its worth and its reality by its effects on the social world. A typical example of this method of approach is W. J. Warner's criticism of Methodism on the ground that, as

[1] See especially Warner, *The Wesleyan Movement and the Industrial Revolution*, and also Ernst Troeltsch, *Social Teaching of the Christian Churches*.
[2] *Religion and the Rise of Capitalism*.

a movement, it failed to translate the Christian ethic of moral responsibility into the social sphere, but concentrated on the individual.[1]

Valuable results have been obtained by such work, and for such historians it must be conceded that this is the natural approach to the problem presented by the attitude of Churchmen to affairs. Along the same line it might be assumed that the attitude of Methodists to political allegiances and programmes would be determined by the extent to which either party's "platform" approximated to Methodist social theory, and that Methodists would follow their founder's advice to take part in politics only when moral issues were concerned, by lending their support to the party with the most comprehensive social programme. It was to be expected that such might happen when issues like slavery, about which Wesley and his followers were uncompromising,[2] were at stake, and when the battle was being fought both in Parliament and in the country by Evangelicals. It might be possible to argue that Methodism was Tory when the social champions, men such as Wilberforce, Oastler, Sadler, and Ashley, were Tories, and that, as the championship of Social Reform passed from benevolent Tories to Radicals and Liberals, so Methodist support swung over to the Left. In this way it might be maintained that Primitive Methodists, and the various Methodists loosely

[1] See Chapter IX on "The Contribution of Wesleyanism to the new Social Values".

[2] This remark applies to England. Although Methodists in America have played a great part in winning the anti-slavery battle there, the question of slavery has caused much trouble and produced schism and dissension in Transatlantic Methodism.

grouped under the adjective "Liberal" or "Free", became politically Liberal more quickly than Wesleyans,
whose social theory, impeded by the bureaucratic conservatism of Conference, lagged behind theirs.[1]

Such speculations are attractive. But political parties
are "multi-interest" parties, and, to find in one of their
aspects the secret of such alignments, seems to involve an
underestimation of the complexity of political relations.
In the twentieth century, politics have become so inter-
mingled with economics and social affairs that it is impossible to separate them; but, in the first generation of
the nineteenth century, political loyalties were not determined according to schemes of social reform put forward
by "Shadow Cabinets". Wilberforce and Shaftesbury
did not choose the Tory party as a medium by which to
realise their dreams; they were Tories who had been
inspired by social ideals. Indeed, then as now, the fundamental division between Tories and Liberals was not one
between rival social theories,[2] but between their allegiance to the rival standards of authority and liberty.
Generally speaking, the Tory has been the authoritarian,
the Liberal the champion of "Freedom", especially for
the individual. Because the M.P.'s of the Clapham sect
were most of them Tories, they believed in the aristocratic dispensation of reform, in reform "from above",
rather than that which might come from basing society
on the "self-directing power of personality", which Pro-

[1] See Henry Carter, *The Social Dynamic and the Methodist
Movement*, especially pp. 9–12.
[2] The Liberal social theory has often been woefully inadequate,
and even Gladstone cannot escape this indictment. *Laissez-faire* has
not always produced social champions!

fessor Hobhouse[1] has defined as the fundamental belief of Liberalism. They were Tories before they were social reformers, and possibly it was for that reason that their activities resulted in Acts of Parliament, for many of the Benthamite Whigs were ill-disposed to use the machinery of the State for social amelioration.

The Toryism of the Clapham sect is interesting, because it furnishes an example of Evangelical philanthropy in politics, and also because its development differed from that of Methodism. The Clapham sect perished, but the Evangelical wing of the Church of England remained predominantly Conservative. Methodism became both Nonconformist and Liberal. The " Saints " were, at least in attitude, aristocrats believing in the ability of the upper classes to give to the lower classes what they needed; the Methodists were mostly members of those lower classes, and they grew to desire that self-government which was anathema to good Tories, but which inspired the enthusiasm for the Reform Bill. Although their religious philanthropy was undoubtedly sincere, there was about many of these aristocratic reformers more than a suspicion of contempt for capitalists, tradesmen, and manufacturers, a contempt fed by the evidence of industrial abuses; many Methodists, rising in the social scale by their success, were themselves becoming members of these classes, and they were led, in part by self-interest, into allegiance with the political party traditionally connected with "Trade". It is more than an historical accident that Evangelical Anglicans should remain Tories, whilst Nonconformists became Liberals.

[1] *Liberalism*, p. 123.

Here may be seen the inadequacy of looking simply to the economic factor for a key to the relation of Methodism with nineteenth-century politics. Such a study of what is essentially Church history must recognise the force of other and more complex considerations. These reformers were reformers because of a religious urge, and they thought religiously—and even politically—before they thought economically. Wilberforce and Shaftesbury alike used their position in the world and in Parliament to express their sense of duty to their fellow-men. Had they thought more economically, they might have attacked the basis of contemporary Society; actually, they attacked definite abuses with a fiery enthusiasm, which issued from passionate convictions rather than from an intellectually conceived Christian ethic. Evangelicalism was not a social theory; one might even say that it had no social theory; but it did set men's hearts on fire with hatred for oppression and with pity for the oppressed. Where it failed it was not simply because it did not "translate the Christian Ethic of moral responsibility into the social sphere",[1] but because it became conventionalised and lost the ardour of its love for men.

Religion and religious ideas had their part in moulding the minds of men, and in determining the way they were to think politically in the tempestuous era preceding the Reform Bill. Most of those whose political consciousness was awakening were members of Churches before they became politicians. It was in accord with tradition that Anglican Evangelicals, with the authoritarian background of a hierarchical Church, should be Tories. Non-

---

[1] *Vide supra*, p. 94.

conformists, with their independent traditions, might be expected to remain loyal to the Whigs. The Methodists, on the borders of Church and Dissent, were not finally settled. According as their Churchmanship was akin to that of one body or the other, they might be expected to reflect in politics the traditional party allegiance of Church or Dissent.

Of the truth of this contention there can be no clear-cut, irrefutable proof. There can, however, be an appeal to the history of Methodism, and of the movements which tore it in the course of the century. From that confused welter of unworthy personal quarrels, inarticulate clamourings after rights withheld, social, economic, political, and spiritual upheavals, the clash of principles far nobler than their champions, may come some answer to the riddle of Methodism's politics. One must return to the history of Methodism itself.

The numerical growth of the Methodist Connexion in the thirty years between the New Connexion quarrel and the Leeds Organ Case was enormous. Every year brought an increase, and numbers grew from 90,347 in 1795[1] to 237,239 in Great Britain in 1827.[2] A temporary check in 1820, when the first decrease in Great Britain amounted to 5388, produced much heart-searching, and the famous "Liverpool Minutes" were

adopted by the Conference held in Liverpool, in the year 1820, on which occasion the enquiry was made,—"What measures can we adopt for the increase of spiritual religion

[1] From 1770 to 1810 quinquennial returns were made: from 1811 annual. See Peirce, pp. 80–3.
[2] There were 294,730 in the whole "British Connexion" in 1827.

among our societies and congregations, and for the extension of the work of God in our native country?"[1]

Methodists lived in a perpetual expectancy that their numbers would grow, and "Revivals" were anticipated as in the natural order of things spiritual.[2]

Methodism was expanding as a Church in this period, and the difference between contemporary methods and those of the eighteenth century is both interesting and important. The old way of societies' growing "by snow-ball action" generally gave place to new ways, whereby great revivals brought thousands into Church membership. The second generation of religious movements tends to use a definite evangelistic technique, and the rigidifying of Methodist orthodoxy had effects alike on piety and on churchmanship.

Lacking a Book of Common Prayer in which to enshrine its devotional genius, Methodism has, ever since the issue of the first collection of the hymns of John and Charles Wesley in 1738,[3] regarded its hymn book as its most precious heritage.[4] More than any other movement, Methodism was responsible for the establishment of a

[1] See Peirce, pp. 791-6, for a copy.
[2] See the stories told of Bramwell and Stoner in *N.H.M.* I, 410-12, and *Lives of the Methodist Preachers*, passim. Stoner's well-known prayer "I am thankful for one soul, but, oh, I want thousands" is typical of the spirit of that period.
[3] 1739 was the date of the first widely used Hymn Book. Other editions followed, until the 1780 Hymn Book became the Standard Collection for the nineteenth century.
[4] Stories are told of Methodist local preachers troubled on their death beds by the realisation that they had "loved their Hymn Books more than their Bibles". Methodists have had their religious ideas influenced by hymns in a manner unparalleled in the history of the Christian Church.

tradition of hymn singing as an integral part of English religion, and consequently it was in its hymns that it most clearly expressed its doctrines. Throughout the nineteenth century most of the hymns sung were those of Charles Wesley, but such hymns as were written during that century seemed to breathe a different atmosphere. It was not only that the nineteenth century produced no Charles Wesley. Much of the freshness, the "Romantic quality",[1] of the early songs of the movement was lost. Expressions which, in the eighteenth century, had been illumined by the light of a new experience came to be used conventionally, and well-nigh automatically, and a comparison of the hymns of nineteenth-century Methodists with those of John and Charles Wesley, Thomas Olivers, and Benjamin Rhodes will show in what way Methodism was changing. The language used was almost identical; the spirit in which it was used had become conventionalised.

Improved means of communication strengthened the Connexional system, and made it possible for Superintendents of Circuits to use the itinerancy, not only to hold together the Societies in their Circuits, but also to hold their expanding Circuits in place in the Connexional machine. Their incessant movement carried revivalism up and down the country, and the great industrial districts became centres of evangelised areas, in which local and itinerant preachers alike pressed fervent appeals upon the working men and shopkeepers who chiefly composed their congregations. New chapels were built,

[1] See Henry Bett, *The Hymns of Methodism in their Literary Relations.*

chapels often far larger than were required, and many a poor Society must have built with the hope that revivals such as those which called it forth would swell its numbers and liquidate the debt it incurred. Chapel debts (one of the curses of a voluntary Church) became a source of constant difficulty in nineteenth-century Methodism.[1] They played no inconsiderable part in leading laymen into an assertion of their rights and of their legitimate position in the Church, and in modifying John Wesley's system of patriarchal Church government. The new Revivalism was not carefully planned, it had not the guiding hand and co-ordinating mind of Wesley, and it issued in an uneconomical spate of chapel building which inundated the young Church with financial embarrassments. It is difficult to see what else could have been done, but we must note this result of the new method. It had repercussions in the next half-century.

Another way in which the revivals affected the Reaction was in the new place assigned to the Church. The essence of the new preaching was individualistic: "An' Muggins 'e preäched o' Hell-fire, an' the loov o' God to men". It directed its twofold appeal to the individual conscience of each hearer, and, like much of the Evangelical religion of the nineteenth and twentieth centuries, it tended to minimise the place of the Church, and to regard as of sole importance the conversion of the individual.

In this it did not follow Wesley. John Wesley realised the importance of individual religion as much as anyone;

---

[1] See Gregory, *Sidelights on the Conflicts of Methodism.*

but he was a truly High Churchman. He recognised the importance of sacraments, and of that fellowship in which Christians could alone live the full Christian life. His "Classes" were to be instruments for the perfecting of "Scriptural Holiness"; they were to provide mutual help for individuals whose witness might otherwise bring them loneliness; they were to be a microcosm of the Church, which was the Body of Christ, and of which they were to be parts. The Methodist system, as John Wesley left it, was a High Church system, and the tests of its membership were intended to be regular attendance at class and demonstration of the fruits of the Spirit in concerted as well as individual activity.

The churchmanship of eighteenth and nineteenth-century Methodists was different. Wesley's disciples formed classes as the early Christians formed their societies,—spontaneously. The converts of the nineteenth-century revivals found societies already formed; they had but to join the Church which had brought about their conversion. They attended class and were loyal Church members, but their allegiance to Methodism was more a matter of course than of spontaneity. Members began to "grow up in the Church of their fathers". The strength of Wesley's organisation held together the converts of a more individualistic evangelism, but it was often a realisation of the strength to be gained from unity and co-operation when rights were to be struggled for that cemented the bonds of the Church. The loyalty of Wesley had been the loyalty of a High Churchman to the Church which is the Body of Christ; the loyalty of the "second generation of Methodists" was that of individualists to a Denomination. John Wesley and his disciples could not think of Christians professing a "solitary religion",[1] and, in consequence, the "Wesleyan Reaction" involved a Protestant interpretation of *Extra Ecclesiam nulla salus*. It was one of the first parts of the Reaction to be modified in the new age when Evangelicalism and Benthamism were, not merely contemporaries, but also twin manifestations of the same individualistic "spirit of the age".[2]

The modification of the "Reaction", due to the introduction of new elements and ideas into original Methodism, proceeded along three main lines. The first of these, represented in the Methodist New Connexion, has been noticed in the previous chapter. Its work was carried on throughout the period, inside both the Old and the New Connexions. The Methodist New Connexion, though always a comparatively small Church,[3] was active, and utterances such as that of the Rev. Thomas Allin at Sheffield in 1833[4] bear testimony to its Liberalism, for Allin was an important and representative man. But the ejectment of 5000 malcontents in 1797 had not removed all the Liberal elements from Wesleyan Methodism.

[1] "Solitary religion is not to be found there (in the religion of Christ). 'Holy Solitaries' is a Phrase no more consistent with the Gospel than Holy Adulterers. The Gospel of Christ knows of no Religion, but Social; no Holiness but Social Holiness." Preface to *Hymns and Sacred Poems*, published by John and Charles Wesley, 1739, pp. viii–ix.

[2] See Dicey, *Law and Public Opinion in England in the Nineteenth Century*, pp. 399–409.

[3] It had only 37,000 members at the time of United Methodist Union in 1907, and in 1814 had only 8292 members with forty-four ministers.

[4] Quoted *supra*, p. 87.

Many remained, and still more came in with the revivals amongst middle and working classes. Many of
them were raw material for Liberalism rather than
actual Liberals, and a combination of circumstances
helped to mould their attitude to both Church and
State.[1]

The thirty years covered by this chapter formed a
period marked by social distress and an awakening political consciousness. Many men who became Methodists
during this period were feeling the pangs of both. With
the freshness of a new discovery, political remedies were
especially attractive. It was an age of faith in such expedients as the Reform Bill and the Charter. The general
Wesleyan attitude to these ambitions was one of hostility.
There were many reasons for this, and not the least important was the fear that, as with the Nonconformists of
a previous epoch, political considerations might weaken
religious ardour. But an official attitude of splendid
isolation from politics could not succeed in weaning men
with grievances from their interest in affairs. Nor could
it quench the ambitions of prospering members of the
middle classes, who, attracted by *laissez-faire*, repelled
by the aristocratic Tories and despised by the Tory
Church of England, were finding in Methodism, with
its abundance of lay offices, outlets not only for their
spiritual, but also for their administrative capacities.

Both discontented working men and "climbing"
bourgeoisie saw in Methodist organisation the germ of a
democratic system. Differing in their conception of
churchmanship from Wesley, they could not appreciate

[1] See Chapter VI.

the paternal character of his ecclesiastical organisation. With Kilham, they looked at what they considered the real democratic spirit of the machine, with its lay officers, trustees, leaders, and stewards. Their churchmanship fostered their nascent Liberalism, as their Liberalism influenced their churchmanship. They were apt to regard pastoral authority as a usurpation of their rights, and if, like Kilham's, their thinking was unhistoric, it was not on that account any less potent a factor in breaking up the "Reaction", and in producing the Methodist Liberal who, a generation later, was to support Gladstone.

The second agent in the disintegration of the Reaction was supplied by the "Ranter"[1] tradition represented by the Primitive Methodists and Bible Christians. Both these movements, the one in the Midlands and the other in the West Country, were fruits of the new spirit and method. The founders of both laid much less stress upon rule and upon propriety than upon passionate preaching and fervent evangelism. They were impatient of restraint and set no store by tradition. Although they remained Methodists, ecclesiastically as well as spiritually, their Methodism was of a modified type.

Church order and regulation were of much less moment than soul-saving and individual edification; these must be attended to whatever became of Church order.[2]

The Primitive Methodist Church sprang from disputes following the prohibition of certain Camp Meetings, first held at Mow Cop in 1807 by the American

[1] This name was given to the Primitive Methodists in Belper as early as 1814, and it has persisted. See *N.H.M.* I, 574.
[2] Rev. H. B. Kendall in *N.H.M.* I, 557.

Evangelist Lorenzo Dow. In 1808 Hugh Bourne, and in 1810 William Clowes, were expelled for their connexion with these irregular meetings. Both of them had followers, and in 1811 they united to form the Primitive Methodist Church, as a Methodist Church in which Connexional regulations should not be allowed to hinder the free moving of the Spirit. Membership of class was still to be the test of church membership, and the " Ranters " were as jealous of their Methodist spirit and origin as were the Wesleyans. Leaders' Meetings, Circuits, District Meetings, and an annual Conference were vital parts of their polity, but there were several differences, due to the different composition of the new Church. The Wesleyan Methodist Church has had a large middle-class membership, but the Primitive Methodist Church has done most of its recruiting from a lower social order, and it has always been predominantly a working-class Church. The simplicity (often crudity)[1] of its preaching has appealed to the labouring classes, and many of the leaders of the Trades Union and Friendly Society movements have been Primitive Methodist local preachers and class leaders.[2] The young Church however did not attract in its early period many of those intellectual artisans who were interested in political theories, or at least it did not supply them with ecclesiastical problems upon which to

[1] Professor Peake's educational work in the twentieth century can scarcely be over-estimated. It has wrought a cultural transformation in Primitive Methodism.

[2] " Ironically enough it was the Methodist local preachers who were the first Labour agitators. (This was especially true of Primitive Methodism, in government the most democratic of all Methodist bodies.)" Edwards, p. 190. See also Sidney Webb, *The Story of the Durham Miner*.

exercise their minds. It had many more members drawn from the ranks of uneducated labourers, and the warmth of their religious fervour gave little room for the heat of ecclesiastico-political controversy.

Moreover, Primitive Methodism has been pre-eminently a layman's Church.[1] Its local preachers have greatly outnumbered its ministers, and laymen have wielded the chief power in the Connexion. The two to one lay to clerical representation in Conference, though a natural expression of the composition of the Church, has added to the laity's strength, and prevented the growth of any strong clericalism. Primitive Methodism was a Nonconformist Methodism, and by no means a High Church movement. Its differences from the "Reaction" are obvious.

The Bible Christians took their origin from the missionary zeal of William O'Bryan in Devonshire. His irregularities brought about his expulsion, and circumstances forced him to set up a new Connexion, closely resembling Kilham's Church in polity. O'Bryan had been influenced by the Quakers,[2] and he introduced important relaxations of Methodist discipline.[3] He claimed a paternal authority akin to Wesley's, but his followers refused to recognise it, and lay representation in Conference was established by the Deed of 1831 "in order to

[1] At the time of Methodist Union in 1932 figures for the Primitive Methodist Connexion were as follows: 222,021 members, 1131 ministers, 12,896 local preachers.
[2] One of the nicknames of the movement was "Quaker Methodists". It was begun in 1815 when the first Society was formed at Lake Farm, Shebbear.
[3] Particularly by the use of a female itinerancy.

prevent priestly domination". The movement was geographically restricted to the West Country, and O'Bryan's chief work was done in Devonshire, a county not much influenced by Wesley. In this area (an area still strong alike in Methodism and in Liberalism) the Wesleyan Reaction was modified by a Liberal constitution and a revivalist $\eta\theta\sigma$.

The third means of modification was internal, and was one of the developments of Wesleyan Methodism itself. In spite of contemporary revivals, Wesleyan Methodism of this period was marked by most of the characteristics usually associated with the second generation of great movements. It was becoming established and recognised *as a denomination*. As a Church with a large and rapidly increasing membership, it was coming to be regarded, by ecclesiastics and politicians alike, as a factor of importance in national affairs. Its attitude was beginning to be studied as such. The organisation of a Church of such a size involved a tightening up of Connexional machinery and an observance of certain fixed rules about its working. This generation saw the establishment of the Connexional system, and its firm foundation as the essential element in Methodist polity. Evangelistically, the period was one of progress, but, constitutionally and doctrinally, as well as politically, it was an age of establishment and of conservatism. Having weathered the New Connexion storm and adjusted itself to the loss of its founder, the second generation looked to the Church's foundations. No new doctrinal standards were set up, and Methodism has been remarkably free from "heresy hunts"; but much greater importance came to be attached to dogmatic orthodoxy.

The evangelical message tended to grow stereotyped, and whenever this happens, evangelicalism becomes ultra-Protestant, alike in its insistence upon individual responsibility and upon Biblical infallibility. This "cooling down process" was attended by important results for that Reaction towards catholic ideals which had marked so much of Wesley's thought and organisation. The departure of Methodism from Wesley's catholic churchmanship was accompanied by a wasting of his sacramental legacy, and each affected the other. When, in the second quarter of the century, the Oxford Movement arose to champion a new Sacramentarianism, Methodists, on this question no less than on others, were ranged with their foremost opponents.

But it was not merely in reaction to "Puseyism" that Methodism forsook its old position. In 1828, Conference had erased, as injudicious, Charles Wesley's words on his mother's tombstone:

> The Father then revealed His Son,
> Him in the broken bread made known.[1]

In the 40 years since the death of the poet, the Church he had helped to establish, and for which he had written his hymns, had moved far. The reason may, paradoxically, be found in the desire not to break with the Church of England; a consideration which had deprived many Methodists of the opportunity for communion for six years between the death of Wesley and the Plan of Pacification,[2] and which, consequently, had caused question-

[1] See Rattenbury, Chapter XVI, p. 180.
[2] "The Lord's Supper shall not be administered by any person among our societies in England and Ireland, for the ensuing year,

ing as to the importance of this practice. It may also be found in the failure of Methodism to develop a Protestant High Churchmanship. Had Methodism, instead of becoming negatively Protestant, wedded its Catholic elements to the doctrine of the Priesthood of All Believers, and allowed, as did the "Minor Methodists", lay administration of the sacraments, or even unrestricted celebration by its separated itinerant ministers, it might have preserved this element of the Reaction and, with it, a really Catholic Free Churchmanship. It had been in the best position to do this; its failure contributed to its gravitation towards Liberalism, by bringing it into line with the Old Denominations.

Financial difficulties wrought important changes in the administration of affairs. The ministerial Conference could not cope with all the debts on the new chapels, and they were anxious to recruit the aid of their wealthier laymen. Influential laymen on the mixed Committee of Privileges[1] had done great service in 1811 in opposing Lord Sidmouth's Bill[2] and causing its withdrawal; whilst they enabled successful lawsuits to be carried through, when Methodists' rights to chapels were called in ques-

on any consideration whatsoever, except in London." *Minutes of Conference of* 1792. The exception in the case of London was due to the fact that Wesley's Chapel, City Road, was served by an ordained Anglican clergyman.

[1] Set up in 1803.

[2] This Bill, introduced into Parliament by the Home Secretary during the Napoleonic Wars, was intended to restrict the provisions of the Toleration Act to ministers of definite congregations. Such a Bill, had it become law, would have withdrawn the benefit of toleration from Methodist ministers, whose itinerancy amongst Societies scattered throughout Great Britain would have disqualified them from holding a licence under the new regulations.

tion. In consequence, they came to be consulted on all matters relating to finance. After several years of experiment, the "Finance District Meeting", to which laymen were invited, was established in 1821. The old principle of invitation was preserved, but, by consulting with laymen about finance, Conference was opening the door to lay claims of a nature not dissimilar from those of Parliament in a previous age. It was one of the first steps in the long and troubled journey to lay representation in Conference, a goal not reached until 1878. The expedients of this period were dictated by practical difficulties, and the "Reaction's" principle of invitation, not of representation, was accepted. But when the tradition of invitation was forgotten the extent of the change in the Reaction became apparent. A system in which the laity, especially of the new type, held the power of the purse, could not permanently remain under sacerdotal rule. The new Methodism contained some semblances at least of potential democracy, and those semblances were seized upon by reformers of a later age.

Yet if there were elements of disintegration and of nascent Liberalism in Methodism at this time, its predominant temper was conservative and authoritarian. In Church government the power of the ministry was greater than ever, and, in 1814, by allowing any minister of fourteen years' standing to be nominated for membership of the "Legal Hundred", Conference increased its vigour. In 1818 Methodist preachers began to use the title "Reverend", and there were many signs that the ministry was becoming increasingly jealous of its privileged position. That position was never seriously challenged during this period, and the clericalism of the "Reaction" was increased rather than diminished by many of the exigencies of a period of revivals, and of the establishment of the Connexional system.

Politically, this hierarchical government was reflected, especially amongst the clerical party, by a strong conservatism. The official attitude to politics was one of non-participation, a course advised by Wesley, who feared that his followers' evangelical faith might be weakened by contact with political affairs. The rigid application of this doctrine had the effect of flinging the weight of Methodism into the scale on the side of reaction and conservatism in the post-war era, for participation in politics meant, for artisans and bourgeoisie alike, supporting movements for the extension of the franchise. When the prerogative of government in the Church was restricted to the ministry, it was natural that such ambitions should have been suspect, and that the ministry should have used its influence against what might ecclesiastically prove dangerous.

There were, however, other factors at work in the building up of the conservatism of Conference at this time, and it is unfair to suspect most of the ministers in Wesleyan Methodism of such political acumen as has been hinted at. Most of them were simple-minded men afraid that the attractions of politics might destroy the faith of their flocks. There were dangers besetting the path of Methodism in the second generation that demanded careful treatment. With the memory of ill-treatment by mobs still fresh, they dared not allow their loyalty to become suspect. The Kilhamites had been assailed as Jacobins, and Conference took care not to fall into the same condemnation. Methodist preachers gave no countenance to the various riots provoked by the general distress; Conference regularly sent addresses of loyalty to the King; many of the large towns had Methodist Chapels called "Brunswick", as a symbol of their unwavering allegiance to the House of Hanover.[1] Their attitude to patriotism was one of scrupulous rectitude, and by it, if they forfeited the respect of the Chartist workingmen,[2] they gained freedom from persecution for the development of the young Church.

The Hammonds[3] have mistaken this attitude of aloofness from politics for a lack of interest in the affairs of the world, but their conclusions are biased and inaccurate.[4] Methodists were concerned with national conditions, but they shrank from associating with atheistical Radicals in overturning an order of society, which, though it might need improvement, could only be reformed by the power of religion. The fate of the " political " Dissenters and the atheism of contemporary Radicals repelled Methodists, and helped to strengthen a conservatism likely to spring from their Church government.

Lastly, Methodism had not adjusted itself to its middle position between the Church and Dissent. The Liberals demanded that it should become openly, as it was be-

---

[1] After the dissensions, many of the United Methodists followed the example of the Wesleyans by naming their chapels "Hanover".

[2] See Faulkner, *Chartism and the Churches*, p. 12.

[3] See *The Town Labourer*, Chapters XI and XIII, and *Lord Shaftesbury*, Chapter XVI.

[4] This criticism applies to almost all their references to Methodism. It is unfortunate that their work should be so marred by preconceived hostilities.

coming practically, a Dissenting Church; Conference clung to the hope of reconciliation with the Church of England. Even when that hope vanished, and Methodism was obviously a separate Church, it remained more friendly to the Anglican than to the Dissenting Churches, as its hierarchical government had more affinities with the Episcopal than with the Independent Churches. In such a case, the pressure of Liberal elements only increased the determination of Conference to remain as neutral as possible.

Its hierarchical government, its fear of the French Revolution, its hatred of Radical Atheism, its dread of the spiritual fate which had befallen such Dissenters as had become deeply implicated in political affairs, its respect for the wishes of its founder, and its desire for reunion with the Church of England, all helped to build up that neutrality in politics, which was the official Wesleyan attitude to politics in this period. Liberal elements, at work below the surface, were, as yet, too weak to stem this rising tide of Conservatism. Their latent force was overborne.

CHAPTER V

"THE POPE OF METHODISM": THE PRIMACY AND POLICY OF JABEZ BUNTING

The history of Methodism in the nineteenth century was moulded by the personality of a great figure. Jabez Bunting was alike a creature and a creator of "Methodism since Wesley", and he was himself the fullest representative of that clerical "Conference party"[1] he welded together during the time of his supremacy. His brethren looked to him for advice and guidance on almost all matters: in theology—he was President of the Theological Institute and his orthodoxy was irreproachable; in Circuit administration—he had framed the "Liverpool Minutes", which set forth the principles of pastoral instruction; in discipline—he was the champion of clerical authority and ecclesiastical rectitude; in politics—as a man of affairs as well as a Connexional leader, his political opinions carried additional weight. In all these matters his supremacy was sufficient to invite comparison between his position and that of John Wesley. The name of "The Pope of Methodism", given to him by his enemies, carried with it at least a semblance of truth, for no other man in Methodism, save Wesley himself, ever exercised so much power, or received so much deference.

[1] This term of abuse was freely used by the Liberal opponents of Bunting.

Bunting was born in the first generation of Methodism; he was cradled, and his ideas were formed, in the second; he himself shaped the third. Between 1803, when he was accepted into full Connexion, and 1856,[1] he only missed one Conference,[2] and the dependence of that body upon him may be surmised from the fact that, on certain occasions when he was absent from sessions, discussion was deferred to a later sitting, that his colleagues might have the benefit of his advice.[3] During the course of his ministerial career he became Editor of the *Wesleyan Methodist Magazine*, Secretary of the Missionary Society (which he did so much to establish), President of the Theological Institute, four times President of Conference, and a member of most of the Connexional Committees, which in this period became increasingly responsible for the most important decisions of the Church.

His power as a preacher had made him Connexionally well known while he was still a young man, and his preaching and his administrative abilities alike increased his fame as he grew older. As his influence and power within Methodism grew, so did his fame outside the Connexion. As a leader of the Evangelical Alliance, as

[1] He died two years later.

[2] That at Leeds in 1830.

[3] "At the morning session of the last Monday of the Conference, Dr Bunting not being present, only small miscellaneous matters were attended to. At last the President proposed the adjournment of the Conference, a very proper suggestion, as in Dr Bunting's absence it appeared that nothing could be done. On the reassembling of Conference, Dr Bunting having returned, business was resumed." Fowler's notes of the 1837 Conference, *Sidelights*, p. 250.

an agitator in the Anti-Slavery movement, and as a
prominent figure in the organisation of missions, he was
the recognised representative of Wesleyan Methodism.[1]
It was not surprising that he should have been regarded
with veneration by his brethren, over whom his
superiority was so obvious.

It is plain...and is admitted by both friends and enemies,
that by the space of forty years Dr Bunting occupied a
perfectly unique position and predominant authority and
influence in the Methodist Connexion, such as no one but the
Founder himself has ever been allowed to wield. Throughout
that period he was, in effect, the Premier, who never went
out of office whosoever might do so, having never been
appointed....It amounted to much more than the being
primus inter pares. During the greater part of the time it
amounted to a veritable Patriarchate or Protectorate.[2]

That position was due in almost equal measure to his
character and to his longevity. He was, in effect, a permanent official of extraordinary ability and forcefulness,
and in a system such as Methodism, his authority was
strengthened by the affection even of those who opposed
him. In more ways than one does he resemble Henry
VIII, and not least because he was a strong man whose
own views so often coincided with those of most of his
colleagues. He may have helped to mould the minds of
successive generations of ministers; he also expressed
many of their convictions, and it was this similarity of
outlook, as much as the continued exertion of his personality, that buttressed his position. Therein lay his secret.

[1] See the standard *Life of Dr Bunting* by his son, T. P. Bunting.
[2] Gregory, *Sidelights on the Conflicts of Methodism*, pp. 527-8.

The theory and practice of a man of such stature was bound to exert a great influence upon the ecclesiastical and political outlook of Methodism. That his most important work was done ostensibly within Methodism cannot hide the developments he wrought in the sphere of national politics, and in his case, perhaps more than in anyone's, can politics be seen as the expression of theological ideas—for it is unjust to attack his churchmanship as nothing more than the theory of an ecclesiastical bureaucrat. His theology was the basis of his thought, and an attempt to appreciate it is essential in any study of Methodism and Politics in the nineteenth century.

That theology had a background. The question of the relations of Methodism with the Anglican Church had exercised the generation of Methodists deprived of Wesley's leadership. They had, at great sacrifice, striven to keep open the door of reunion, but circumstances had rendered their efforts unavailing. Bunting grew up in a Society which had become a separate Church, and which was no longer an outcrop of Anglicanism. Like Kilham, Bunting took seriously his Dissenting Minister's licence,[1] and his refusal of a better-paid curacy in Macclesfield in 1802[2] was an expression of his belief in the independent existence of Methodism, even more than of hostility to the National Church. Like Kilham, he could not be content to regard Methodism as tied to the Church of England, but unlike Kilham, he did not logically demand that she should become one of the sects. Methodism had been forced into an independent position midway be-

[1] In 1805 he was saved from the press-gang by his licence.
[2] T. P. Bunting, pp. 137-9.

tween the Church and the Nonconformists, and in that middle position Bunting was resolved she should remain. He had no patience with "anti-State-Church" agitations, and he desired Methodism to preserve a position of impressive but friendly detachment from these disputes. Methodism's work must be a nobler one than that of making political protests against the privileges of a body of fellow-Christians. Methodism might lose its evangelical fervour, as "Political Dissent" had done, if it were led into such controversies.

His views were expressed clearly at the trial of Joseph Rayner Stephens, the Chartist leader, who was expelled from Conference for his persistent connexion with a Lancashire "Church Separation Society" in 1834:

> Let us not take off our hand from the work he [John Wesley] has left us to complete and lay it destructively upon that adjoining house, even though it be an eyesore. We can live in our own house and do as we please....He was nearer to the Church than to Dissent. And that is our position practically. Perhaps we should be neutral....Our principle is "*Dissent when we must*, but be on friendly terms when we can".[1]

In his relations with the National Church, his policy supplied an illustration of his famous aphorism, in some ways the most illuminating remark he ever made: "We stand stock still". A measure of "freedom" had come to Methodism in the second generation, and, upon that, the architect of the third generation wished to build the new Church. Such a legacy was not to be wasted, but to be

---

[1] *Sidelights*, pp. 155–6. The italics are Fowler's. *Sidelights* is based on Fowler's Journal. For its reliability see Bunting's expression of confidence quoted on p. 4.

embodied in the structure. Methodism was to be a Free Church rather than a Dissenting Church.

If Methodism was to stand "stock still", its relation to other religious bodies was bound to change. In spite of itself it was drawn further away from Anglicanism. The Scottish Disruptions revealed the dangers of an Established Church, and Bunting, who was a friend of Dr Chalmers, sympathised with the Free Church party. Such connexions weakened his regard for the English Establishment, and the rise of the Tractarian Movement further strained the relations between Methodists and Evangelicals. In the course of a speech at the Manchester Conference in 1841 on a plan of reunion submitted by a clergyman, he said:

No person on earth or in heaven—if I may use the language —can reconcile Methodism with High Churchism. I have always said that amalgamation is impossible. I wish the Evangelicals would disavow the Puseyites. When Mr Wesley was alive something ought to have been done; but not now. We must now maintain a separate and distinct position, and yet hope that the time may come for a more formal union to be effected. But we must look toward the millennium. At present it is not practicable nor, in our circumstances, desirable (*Loud Cheers*). Unless the Church of England will protest against Puseyism in some intelligible form, it will be the duty of the Methodists to protest against the Church of England. I have said this to the first men in the land.[1]

This altered attitude toward Anglicanism did not involve Dissenting Liberalism; but it prepared the way for it, when other factors had brought about the change which made Methodism the greatest of the Free Churches.

[1] *Sidelights*, p. 317.

That change did not come during the period covered by this essay; but the factors which produced it ripened then. Paradoxically enough, Jabez Bunting helped forward the ripening process.

Against this background must be considered Dr Bunting's most important theological ideas concerning the place and power of the ministry. In this sphere Bunting may be said to have developed one of John Wesley's ideas. It was, however, as much a "Buntingian" as a "Wesleyan" idea. The doctrine of ministerial authority and pastoral supremacy he held, as he held all his beliefs, firmly and positively. He believed it to be in accord with New Testament teaching and, as such, binding upon Methodism. "Christ has given the members to the Pastors in a sense in which they are not given to the Leaders."[1] That was the basic doctrine of his "Pontificate".

Although their sacramentarianism, their ritualism, their Romanism (for many of the early leaders eventually found their spiritual home in Rome), their setting up of tradition alongside the Bible as the basis of authority, and their "unchurching" of their opponents were anathema to Bunting, it is strange to read a letter written in 1828, by this uncompromising opponent of the Tractarians:

All things considered [the question asked was one concerning the advisability of the public admission of new members into Church fellowship] it is questionable whether, under any form, the old quiet, unostentatious practice of Methodism be not much safer than the innovation, which I fear originated in the days of..., who were then full of the Kilhamist theory, and have imbibed the Dissenting principle, that not the

[1] *Sidelights*, p. 191.

pastor, but *the Church* collectively, should have the power of the keys.[1]

Newman's advice to the clergy to "magnify their office" had a parallel in Methodism.

Had prejudice not blinded his eyes, Bunting might have seen in "Puseyism" many of his own most cherished ecclesiastical ideals, but he would never have subscribed to its sacerdotal dogmas. Bunting's clericalism was, in fact, a doctrine of paternal rather than of priestly government. As President of Conference in 1828, he enunciated this principle in another letter:

The superintendent in our economy is the man directly responsible to God, and to the Conference, and to the Connexion, for every department of Methodistical service in the Circuit placed under his care. Having the whole ultimate responsibility he must have correspondent authority: and that necessarily implies that the supreme direction of the whole work must be vested in his hands, checked and guarded indeed, but still sufficiently strong to answer the purposes of a good and efficient government. He is the father of the family, and must have paternal rule over the whole household. He is the general-in-chief, and must judge of the disposal of all his troops.[2]

There could be little sympathy between such fundamentally different attitudes to the ministry as those of the "Pope of Methodism" and the Pope of Rome: Jabez Bunting was an authoritarian rather than a sacerdotalist. Herein lay one of the modifications he introduced into the Wesleyan Reaction, a modification which not only undermined the Reaction, but which, by canalising and

---

[1] *Life of Dr Bunting*, II, 251.   [2] *Ibid.* p. 252.

"materialising" the theory, prevented the evolution of that "High Protestantism" which Methodism was particularly qualified to produce.[1]

With these ideas as his inspiration, it was natural that Bunting should do all in his power to exalt the position of the "separated ministry". The sanctioning of the title "Reverend" (1818), the institution of a "Pastoral Address" (1819), the establishment of a theological institute (1835), and, after he had tactfully pushed forward the idea for several years, the revival of the practice of ordination by laying-on of hands (1836), are all traceable either to his influence or to ideas in accord with his own. All these innovations were symptoms of the growth of a self-conscious clericalism, whose leader and inspiration was the "master mind" of Methodism.

The repercussion of this theory upon laymen's rights was interesting. Laymen were, through the financial door, finding their way into most of the spheres of Connexional activity, but the new exaltation of the ministerial order was calculated to counteract any resultant improvement in their position in the Connexion. Stress was laid by the "clericals" upon the fact that laymen were *invited* to co-operate with the ministers in the government of the Church, and that they had no *rights* to office. The champions of the pastorate sometimes absurdly minimised the importance of lay officers: trustees, though necessary, were devoid of concern for spiritual matters, local preachers were "local talkers", and Class Leaders and Circuit Stewards the mere nominees of Superintendents who were "Angels of the Church". Even the debt which

---

[1] See *supra*, p. 110.

Methodism owed to John Wesley's novel use of lay agencies in his work was minimised by the substitution (in 1822), in Wesley's memorial tablet in the City Road Chapel, of the phrase "chief promoter and patron of the plan of itinerant preaching", for "patron and friend of Lay Preachers, by whose aid he established the plan, etc."[1]

Jabez Bunting was defended against the attacks of the "Liberal" Methodists on the grounds that he had been responsible for almost all the reforms by which the laity gained admission to Connexional government, and the claim was just. That he emphasised lay subordination to the pastorate was equally true. He was afraid of the power of numbers and the purse over-weighing spiritual considerations, and he was convinced that:

The true and scriptural authority of the ministry must on no account be blinked or compromised in these latitudinarian days.[2]

One of the key words in Bunting's vocabulary was "Centralisation". With his theory of ministerial authority he found to his hand an instrument through which it might be expressed. In 1814 he had been the first man elected by nomination into the "Hundred", which was still the nucleus of Conference, and it had been on his suggestion that it was resolved in that year to fill every fourth vacancy by nomination from amongst ministers of

[1] S. D. Waddy's Report in 1881, p. 119, quoted by A. Burbridge, S.J., in *Wesleyanism* (Catholic Truth Society), p. 30. This generation seemed fond of defacing inconvenient memorials. Cf. *supra*, p. 109.

[2] Letter to Beecham on his *Essay on Wesleyan Polity*, quoted in *Life*, II, 258.

at least fourteen years' standing.[1] The reform was calculated to infuse vigour into the "Hundred", and to make Conference the goal of ministerial ambitions. Bunting was, throughout his career, the champion of Conference, and the reform of 1814 was only one of the ways in which he strove to extend its power in every part of the Connexion.

If the sting of the *Fly Sheets*[2] was in their truth, they stung nowhere more effectively than in their attacks upon "Centralisation and Location".[3] They were there criticising the most obvious results of Bunting's policy, a policy which had led him to that office in London, whence he controlled Connexional affairs. In all things he strove to act in the name of Conference, and, if the *Fly Sheets* were unjust in their ascription to him of purely selfish motives, there was no doubt about his coveting of power for Conference. The soul of resistance to any suggestions for decentralisation (except in purely temporal matters), he did everything in his power to make Conference, not only the sovereign body in the constitution (the Deed Poll of 1784 had determined that) but omnicompetent. The basis of the charges of "Popery" was his effort to exalt the Conference, for his enemies sceptically believed that he was using it as a cloak for his own arbitrary power, that, like Henry VIII, he chose to act through a subservient body, rather than to shoulder the sole responsibility for unpopular measures. He certainly was able to

[1] The old method had been by seniority, and it still applied to three in every four vacancies.

[2] See *infra*, Chapter VII.

[3] *F.S.* No. 1 was headed "On Location, Centralization, and Secularization".

carry Conference with him in most of his projects, and the opposition to him was rarely able to do more than protest against measures carried by overwhelming majorities.[1] However the personnel of the combatants might vary, in the conflicts of Methodism throughout the course of well nigh half a century there was one undaunted leader, whose party was not inaptly nicknamed the "Conference party".

Bunting was a true paternalist in his attitude to the relations between Conference and "the People". Although he had introduced lay members into Connexional committees, he was resolutely opposed to their admission into the highest court in the Church. The people's rights, he held, were as adequately protected by the wisdom of their pastors as they could be by the presence of delegates of their own choosing, whilst a clerical Conference, being more homogeneous, would be a more efficient instrument of government. His policy was an honest application of his beliefs.

Would it not be well to go a little more largely into the *reasons* which prevent the Conference from admitting lay delegates into its assembly, and to show that it is not mere lust of power, but an enlightened regard to our pastoral trust, and to the purity of our doctrines and ministry, and to the preservation of itinerancy, and to the real welfare and liberty of the *people at large*, that makes us object to a *mixed* Conference?[2]

He was no admirer of Nonconformity, and he hoped, by centralising the government of the Church, to avoid

[1] See *Sidelights, passim*.
[2] Letter to Dr Beecham, quoted in full in *Life*, II, 256–8. This letter contains some of the most illuminating revelations of Dr Bunting's views on Church government.

the danger of local interests interfering with breadth of vision—a danger he saw only too clearly amongst the Independents, and a danger which the United Methodist Free Churches later found was no illusory one. This aspect of his policy reveals one of the most far-sighted elements in his hatred of democracy. He believed the pastorate to be free, alike from subservience to local interests, owing to the itinerancy, and from the narrowness of view which was likely to prevail amongst laymen. In the interests of the people themselves he advocated centralisation.

His desire to centralise the Church was closely linked with his dogma of the divine authority of the Christian ministry. In Methodism, the authority of the ministry was bound up with that of Conference, in a manner almost akin to the Catholic connexion of clerical authority with the historic episcopate. The Methodist ministry was organised as a collective pastorate, a type of ecclesiastical government with a parallel only in the "Apostolate" of the Early Church.[1] The principle of the itinerancy hindered the growth within the Methodist Societies of any Independent ideas about pastoral authority being based upon separate congregations; and it demonstrated to Circuits the fact that their ministers were members of an order in the Church, and that that order had the disposal of patronage. It was the Stationing Committee which had the "allocation of Circuits", and the wishes of Circuit or preacher alike must bow to the ruling of Conference, through which most clearly and decisively the collective pastorate spoke.

[1] See Workman, *Methodism in the Catholic Church*, pp. 97–101.

Bunting was jealous for the preservation of this peculiarly Methodist usage, and his exaltation of Conference[1] was one of the ways in which he strove to buttress Methodist tradition against the encroachments of democratic, dissenting, and lay elements in the Connexion. He would tolerate no attempts to modify this government by divine right of Conference. On behalf of a bureaucratically led clerical aristocracy, he invoked the authority of John Wesley and of the New Testament alike to refute his opponents. In all the struggles which tore Methodism in the second quarter of the nineteenth century, the one constant issue involved was this right of the joint pastorate to govern, through the Conference and its nominees, the whole of the affairs of Methodism.

In Dr Bunting's policy, by which he says "I mean my course of action", the supreme authority of the Pastorate was, to all practical intents and purposes, the *Constitution* underlying all documentary elements, whether settlements, *plans of pacification*, reciprocal regulations, enactments of the Conference or what not. If at any time any such settlements, plans, regulations, enactments, precedents, or what else, should hamper or imperil that supreme authority, *they*, not *it*, must give way....

All these petitions [for an authorised explanation of our rules] we have seen, Dr Bunting steadily resisted and successfully staved off. Anything like a digest, codification, or authorised compendium he instinctively eschewed. If the Constitution and the law be definitively explained by the authority itself in such wise as to shut out all ambiguity or

[1] See his sentiments on the allocation of stations in 1804: "Now 'who shall decide when Doctors disagree?' My answer is, God, and the Conference, who to me, in this business, are God's representatives." *Life*, I, 260.

possibility of two opposed constructions, then the meaning of
a law can no longer be determined by the action of the Conference; but, on the contrary, the action of the Conference must
itself be determined by its own explanation of the Constitution
and the law.[1]

He had scant sympathy with Whig respect for either
abstract rights or "written constitutions". He was more
than a bureaucrat; he was the Methodist apostle of
pastoral supremacy.

The churchmanship of both John Wesley and Jabez
Bunting brought upon them charges of "Popery", but
they were "Popes" of very different types. Both men
were autocrats, but, whilst Wesley's authority held his
Societies together, Bunting's produced a loss of 100,000
members in five years (1850–5). Those facts point to the
chief difference between the two men. Wesley claimed
loyalty to himself as to the "Father of his People";
Bunting to the system of which he was the directing
genius. Wesley, though spiritually a High Churchman,
was content to throw aside the system, and "to be more
vile"[2] in order to save souls; Bunting, without Wesley's
spiritual depth, and with a less adequate conception of
the Church, wished to mould Methodism according to a
concrete model. The real difference between the two was
a difference between a spiritual and a material High
Churchmanship: Wesley's was the ascendancy of a saint,
Bunting's the ascendancy of a masterful ecclesiastic.
Jabez Bunting has no true place beside John Wesley in
the "Wesleyan Reaction".

[1] *Sidelights*, pp. 499–500.
[2] *Journal*, April 2nd, 1739, where Wesley explained the reasons
which led him to adopt the method of "field preaching".

In politics, Bunting was a strong Tory, and this Toryism was the natural expression of his ecclesiastical authoritarianism. It was strengthened by contemporary circumstances, for he was carried along in that reaction against the French Revolution which engulfed English politics in the early nineteenth century. He heard, in that Revolution, all the political shibboleths that he hated. The political controversies and fears of French invasion, in which he had been cradled in Manchester, had nourished these antipathies. Revolution had meant war, disorder, licence, misery, contempt for all forms of authority, and, above all, godlessness. Its chief exponents in England were either Atheists, like Tom Paine, or Unitarians, like Price and Priestley, and it was Unitarianism which had sapped much of the life of English Nonconformity. The connexion of the two was in itself almost enough to prejudice contemporary Methodists against a movement, from which it was constitutionally averse, and with which unscrupulous enemies tried shrewdly, though unjustly, to link it in the public mind.

Lord Sidmouth's Bill of 1811[1] revealed the danger of this misunderstanding. The Toryism of contemporary Methodism was not only an expression in politics of its ecclesiastical ideals and of its friendliness to the Church of England, but it was also one aspect of its attempt to achieve national recognition and respectability. Without his aristocratic and purely clerical ideas, it was a Toryism akin to John Wesley's own, but it had lost those Liberal elements of its founder's political faith, which had made him more of an independent than a consistent Tory.

[1] *Vide supra*, p. 110 n.

Bunting reflected this development, and, as he was the greatest authoritarian of them all, so was he the completest Tory. He hated the Radicals, both in their ideals and their practice; his methodical, bureaucratic mind shrank instinctively from disorder or revolution; he hoped to preserve Methodism from such entangling alliances as those which had robbed of their spiritual heritage so many of the Whig Nonconformists; and he could see no good likely to issue from political reforms, either for Methodism or for the nation. Politically, as well as ecclesiastically, he seems to have had for his motto: "We stand stock still".

When the political activity of many of the men, from whom Methodism was recruiting at this time, took the form of Radicalism or Chartism in the lower classes, and agitation for electoral reform amongst the middle classes, one result of Bunting's policy was an attempt to purge Methodism of these obnoxious elements. The preachers attacked the Luddites and the Chartists alike, the Wesleyan ministers took no part with their Dissenting brethren in presenting petitions either for the extension of the franchise or for the repeal of the Corn Laws. Many "Liberals" left Wesleyan Methodism to find a more hospitable shelter in Primitive Methodism, and in the various bodies which seceded during the period of the dissensions. Many more were expelled for their association with political causes, especially in the north-east, where Radical classes had been formed.[1]

Bunting led the Connexion in opposition to these developments, and he was probably responsible for drawing

[1] See *Life*, II, 166 *et seq.*

up the letter from the Committee of Privileges enjoining loyalty to the King and government, and forbidding Methodists to become members of Radical societies. His biographer admits that these circumstances "subsequently influenced materially some secessions from the parent body",[1] for they made a great section of the Church, and one which was particularly susceptible to contemporary Radical and Liberal dreams, feel that the clerical party was unsympathetic towards the natural political aspirations of a newly self-conscious class. The attitude of Bunting and his party to Trade Unionism and Parliamentary Reform alike was a contributory factor, not only in developing the Conservative elements inherent in Methodism, but in the stiffening of what Liberal opposition remained. That the great Liberal Methodist revolt of 1849 was predominantly a movement of laymen drawn from the new "Liberal" classes, and that the Wesleyan Reformers were strong Liberals in politics, were results that bore the mark of Jabez Bunting's influence.

His interpretation of the "No Politics Rule" gave cause for grievance; for, whilst he and Robert Newton were allowed, almost unchallenged, to support Tory candidates,[2] Liberals like Thomas Galland were censured for writing political letters to the press,[3] and Radicals were expelled from many Wesleyan Methodist

[1] *Life*, II, 169.
[2] See *Sidelights*, pp. 165–6, and p. 202. Lord John Russell was deeply hurt by his defeat at Tavistock in 1834, a reverse which he ascribed to Methodist influence.
[3] The paper in this case was *The Leeds Mercury*. See *Sidelights*, pp. 237 *et seq.*

Societies. Bunting had the support of all earnest Methodists in his resolve to keep politics of any sort out of the pulpit (and the decrease of membership in 1831 was attributed to the influence of the political disturbances of that year), but the open Toryism of his public life, the unequal treatment of offenders against the " No Politics Rule", and the arrogant manner in which he repelled the attacks of his critics, making all remarks on the matter into issues of " No Confidence",[1] warranted Beaumont's observation: " My difficulty is with the brethren who, whilst gagging others, say and do what they please"[2].

Whether intentionally or not, the "Primate's" administration of this rule, and there were few spheres where his power was less limited, resulted in the encouragement of a conservatism, which is always the concrete form of political quietism, and in a corresponding resentment amongst his opponents. He carried with him the majority of Wesleyan Methodists; but he roused the hatred of those Radicals and Liberals who saw in his power, and in the system he personified, the thwarting of all their cherished hopes, political as well as ecclesiastical. Authoritarianism, whether in Church or State, was anathema to them; it was at the core of Bunting's thought and practice. It was his inspiration in building a structure which might resist the rising tide of democracy—" Methodism hates Democracy as much as it hates Sin"—but, when the flood burst the dam in 1849, the ruin was never repaired. In the devastation which followed, the remains

[1] See *Sidelights, passim*. This was one of Bunting's gravest faults.
[2] *Sidelights*, p. 166.

of the "Wesleyan Reaction" were washed away, and Methodism prepared to build a new abode upon the Nonconformist bank, and, albeit slowly, to be influenced by the Liberal alliance of its neighbours.

Although Jabez Bunting's most far-reaching work was done inside his own Connexion, he was, not only as a Wesleyan, but also as an Evangelical, a prominent public figure. He took the lead in all public matters of concern to Wesleyans, and acted as their representative in questions affecting Missions, Slavery Abolition, Roman Catholic Emancipation, Sabbath Observance, Disestablishment, and Education. On questions affecting Parliamentary Reform, the Corn Laws, and Free Trade, he was, for so prominent a public man, strangely quiet. His reticence is significant, for it points to the real nature of Bunting's interest in affairs. He was not a politician. His approach to public questions was that of a Churchman, not that of a man of affairs interested in the relation between religion and politics. In spite of his thoroughly Tory sympathies, he could only be drawn into political controversies when he saw them as religious questions. He was comparatively unconcerned about the theoretical rights or wrongs of Disestablishment. He had no real quarrel with the Church of England, he disliked her opponents, and he resented the wasting of spiritual energies on so negative a controversy. The issue was not sufficiently vital to excite his interest, and to the dead weight of Wesleyan inertia in the era of the Reform Bill the Establishment owed its persistence.

Other questions he regarded in a similar manner, and even Education, which, as an issue in the nineteenth century, deeply influenced Nonconformist politicians, was not, with Bunting, anything other than a fundamentally religious problem. He was concerned with the adequacy of facilities for Biblical teaching, and with the relations between the various denominations, rather than with the social, political, and economic aspects of the problem. In this he represented faithfully the new spirit Evangelicalism introduced into politics. The Whigs, used to Dissenting support of old, could not appreciate the difference the Revival had made. Misunderstanding the minds of the Wesleyans in particular, they blundered into opposition. Like modern social historians of the period,[1] they approached their problems socially or politically, and they could not understand the scruples of philanthropists and social reformers whose thought forms were primarily religious. It would be a mistake to look for the roots of contemporary Methodist Conservatism in its attitude to contemporary issues; Jabez Bunting's public utterances were expressions of a deeply rooted philosophy which ran through every department of his thought, and which was stamped upon the ecclesiastical and political life of his Church. In the second half of the century, when Methodism and Liberalism had been wedded, social and political issues came to be treated as more important, but it would be anachronistic to look for this concern in the formative period of Methodism. It is for this reason that the contemporary educational

[1] In the case of the Hammonds this lack of sympathy results in an under-estimation of the work done by Evangelicals and Methodists. It is a mistake to think of nineteenth-century religion as merely eschatological or sabbatarian. Those were but two of many elements.

controversies have received so little consideration in this examination of Methodism and Politics down to 1851.

Jabez Bunting's effect upon the outside world was due to his ascendancy and activity as a representative of Wesleyan Methodism. For all practical purposes his voice was the oracle of Wesleyanism, his *ex cathedra* pronouncements seemed almost akin to papal bulls, and, as there were few inside the Connexion who dared to contradict him, so there were few outside it who heard representative voices other than his. It was little wonder that the Tory agents in *Coningsby* thought of the "respectable Wesleyans" as useful allies in the 'thirties and 'forties. Not only could they see this feature in the localities, but they were unlikely to hear any Wesleyan voice other than Bunting's or Newton's. Liberal voices remained local murmurs in Leeds and the north, at least so far as the world might hear them. There was no means of calculating the comparative strength of the two sides, so the Toryism of Jabez Bunting was accepted by the world as a faithful reflection of Methodism's attitude to politics.

Social historians have found it easy to exaggerate the conservatism of Methodism, because the limelight which fell upon the career of Bunting left so much of the rest of the stage in darkness. Even if one admits his representative character, and there can be little doubt that contemporary Methodism was predominantly Tory in sympathy, that does not render any less real the Radicalism of Primitive Methodists, and the essential Liberalism of the New Connexion Methodists and Wesleyan Reformers of 1849. To trace the genesis of the Methodist Liberals one has to use sidelights, as well as limelights. Most important

of all, one must approach the problem, not from outside, as a politician, but from inside, where personal
relations and ecclesiastical and theological ideas were
moulding both the political and the religious lives of
men and women.

It was here that, in every sphere, Jabez Bunting's influence was greatest. He was the leader of nineteenth-
century Wesleyan Methodism, and, in spite of opposition,[1] he forced much of his policy upon the Church. As
a bureaucrat, he received the deference due to an expert
in ecclesiastical affairs, and he succeeded in carrying
Conference and the Church with him in his reforms of
administration. The centralisation of government and
the supremacy of the joint pastorate, which marked
Wesleyan Methodism by the middle of the nineteenth
century, were directly due to his leadership. He was a
"Father" of his Church and an architect of its government, but his policy led to the most disastrous chapter
in that Church's history. For good and for ill, Jabez
Bunting's was the policy that moulded contemporary
Methodist affairs. He was, as his enemies called him,
a veritable "Methodist Pope".

[1] See *Sidelights, passim*, for the nature of this opposition and his
way of overriding it.

CHAPTER VI

POLITICS AND THE LAITY: OPPOSITION TO THE CONFERENCE PARTY, 1827-46

The second quarter of the nineteenth century has usually been regarded by historians as the "Dark Age" of Methodism. It was the era of the great disruptions, which not only rent the Church, but which seemed at one time almost to have destroyed its spiritual life. Before 1827 there had only been one important secession from Wesleyan Methodism—that of Kilham's New Connexion. The other Methodist Connexions, such as the Primitive Methodists and the Bible Christians had set up, had been new developments rather than "schisms". Far from weakening Methodism, they had added to its strength in new areas and amongst new social classes. In the period covered by this chapter, however, the conflicts of Methodism were ecclesiastical in origin and divisive in effect. Their roots lay deep in the life of the Church itself, and their branches cast a shadow over almost every Circuit in Wesleyan Methodism.[1] It was part of the price paid for an efficient Connexionalism that disturbances could rarely be localised, and when the final catastrophe of

[1] It is interesting to note that it was in Circuits where there were contemporary revivals that the disturbances took least effect. In such places (many of them were in country districts) spiritual considerations weighed more heavily than ecclesiastical, and men were left less time to devote to theoretical questions of "rights".

138

1849–51 occurred, it robbed Wesleyan Methodism of more than one-quarter of its actual Church members.[1]

It was a sad end to the "Pontificate". For half a century Bunting had worked to build and consolidate a great Church with a doctrine of Pastoral Supremacy; he lived to see that Church rent from top to bottom, and "Pastoral Supremacy" anathematised by 100,000 Methodist "exiles". His policy destroyed the very unity it was intended to bring to the Church. He had been supreme amongst his brethren, but he had aroused the hatred and the opposition of many of the most influential and numerous classes in the Church. He had championed the rights, as he had determined the policy, of the clerical Conference, but he had not been at such pains to cultivate the good will of those laymen of the middle and working classes who were to form the strength of the nineteenth-century Liberal party. Bunting's *ex cathedra* fulminations against democracy might impress his clerical brethren, and convince the world of the Conservatism of Methodism (the world has always tended to think of "Wesleyanism" and "Methodism" as synonymous), but they could not destroy the political and ecclesiastical ideals of Methodist laymen.

It would be a mistake to regard Methodist history in terms of one man's supremacy. For thirty years, Methodism may have borne Jabez Bunting's head on its obverse side,[2] but, on the reverse, was a new class, quickened and inspired by Methodism, rising in the social and economic

---

[1] In addition to "adherents".
[2] In many books the portrait of Bunting is given in profile as on a coin.

scale, and becoming an active political force. If one side attracted more attention than the other, both were faces of the same coin; Jabez Bunting and Wesleyan Methodism were not alternative terms. The "Pope of Methodism" was opposed, both inside and outside Conference, by men whose thinking did not coincide with his, and who were not always overawed by his personality. He was usually successful in realising his objects, but he did not always carry the whole Church with him. To achieve the purpose of this essay it is as important to study the reverse of the coin as the obverse, to trace the latent forces of Liberalism as to examine the patent Conservatism of Conference.

Although it is not easy to estimate the extent of the Methodist laity's interest in contemporary politics, there are at least two suggestive "pointers": the continual re-iteration by Conference of the "No Politics Rule", and the ascription to politics of the reason for declines either in fervour or in numbers. Rules which are well observed do not need constant restatement, and the frequency with which Bunting made known his adherence to this part of "Mr Wesley's Plan" does not indicate a state of perfect obedience, either amongst the ministers or amongst the laymen. Whilst Methodism, as a Church, escaped many of the dangers of political entanglements, it was not able to keep all its members immune.

The interest of Methodists in Trades Unions and Friendly Societies has already been noticed.[1] Another form of social and semi-political activity became pre-

[1] *Vide supra*, p. 106. Loveless, the leader of the "Tolpuddle Martyrs", was a Methodist local preacher.

valent in this period, with the rise, in 1832, of the Total
Abstinence Movement. Livesey and Anderton, two of the
" Seven Men of Preston ", were Methodists, and earnest
artisan Methodists joined the " Teetotal " movement to
make an uncompromising protest against the evils they
saw around them. The Bible Christians in the west
country and Primitive Methodists in the midlands and
north-east were apostles of the movement. Wesleyan
Methodism was however true to its traditions, and
frowned upon this new social venture. The noisy
meetings and Radical tendencies of the Teetotallers
alarmed Conference, which, in 1841, passed the resolu-
tions:

1. That no unfermented wines be used in the administration of the Sacrament throughout the Connexion.

2. That no Wesleyan Chapel be lent for the meetings of
the Temperance Society.

3. That no preacher shall go into another Circuit to advocate teetotalism without the sanction of the Superintendent
of the Circuit to which he may be invited.[1]

The reason for this action was the same as that which
had ranged Conference against the Trades Unions and
Friendly Societies. Not only did such activities interfere
with the normal functions of the Church, but they tended
to become the centres of political hopes and interests. If
Anderton be taken as typical of these social enthusiasts,
there seem to have been grounds for the suspicion. He
was a Parliamentary Reformer whose political appetite

[1] Quoted in Allen, *Methodism and Modern World Problems*. See
Sidelights, p. 318, for an account of the debate on this motion.

had been whetted in 1832. He desired Universal Manhood Suffrage, and

> declared himself to be the friend of universal freedom, and especially the emancipation of the working classes. To secure this liberty he would give every man of sound mind and good morals a vote, and he would protect that vote by ballot.[1]

He had, in fact, become an abstainer because of the drinking in his Reform club.[2] The Bible Christian and Primitive Methodist Churches had no disciplinary rules against the political activity of their members; but, if the Wesleyan Methodist Church were to keep clear of politics, it would be necessary to avoid any official contact with the Total Abstinence movement. It could not, however, prevent its lay members becoming active supporters of the societies springing up throughout the country. The revolution in Methodism's official attitude to this, as to other similar social questions, worked from within, and reflected its internal condition. Methodist laymen were, on such questions, often ahead of their pastors.

A contemporary political movement which recruited from the Methodist laity was that collection of political remedies for economic ills—Chartism. The Hammonds have noted the formation of "Chartist Churches"[3] and the number of Methodists in them; Methodism itself had its Chartist and Radical classes, especially on the

---

[1] Pilkington, *Methodism in Preston and its connexion with the Temperance and Teetotal Movements.*

[2] It is worthy of note that Anderton was a "Reformer" before he became interested in the social question of drunkenness.

[3] *Age of the Chartists*, pp. 251–2.

north-east coast. Conference, through the Superintendents, tried to suppress the movement, but it could not
be eradicated, and it was merely driven to work below
the surface. The working classes had had their natural
English distrust of the State strengthened by the Combination Acts, and now their resentment was turned
also against their ministers, whom they regarded as Tory
supporters of an oppressive *régime*. They had hoped that
the Great Reform Bill of 1832 would have been but the
first step towards that system of universal franchise which
was to change the character of the State, and, in accord
with Liberal ideals, to extend the sphere of liberty by the
contraction of that of government; they now saw, in
their own ministers, opponents of their most cherished
ambitions. Events of this kind were bound to have their
effect upon the formation of an anti-clerical party within
Methodism, and they helped to link anti-clericalism with
the new political Liberalism. It was this union of political
aspirations with a growing resistance to the claims of the
pastorate that was chiefly responsible for the Liberalism
of the Methodist laity in the second quarter of the nineteenth century.

The "Hungry Forties" made Free Trade a political
issue of vital import. The working classes were rallied
against the Corn Laws, which manufacturers and the
bourgeoisie generally disliked as "in restraint of trade",
and as increasing the cost of production. Nascent Liberalism was provoked to action because the Tories were
regarded as the champions of the aristocratic landed
interest. Wesleyan Methodism officially stood aloof from
the Anti-Corn Law movement, but Bunting's letter, re-

fusing to help in the agitation, contained his approval of the reform. Methodist laymen, especially in Lancashire, did not follow the official example. Many of them were cotton manufacturers and shopkeepers, who realised the advantages which would accrue, both to themselves and to the artisan and labouring classes, if the movement led by Bright and Cobden should succeed. They could not be restrained from taking part in demonstrations and propaganda, and their Superintendents were not always inclined to rebuke wealthy trustees and office-holders for participation in a movement with which many of them sympathised. Chapel debts were often too heavy to admit of the " No Politics Rule " being rigorously enforced against the men best able to bear the Church's financial burdens.

The growth of a Free Trade party was no inconsiderable factor in determining the political allegiance of Methodism's industrial bourgeoisie, and, although the economic factor assumed greater importance in the second half of the century, it was beginning, at this time, to exercise a definite influence amongst the manufacturing classes. The ranks of Methodism were swelled by manufacturers, shopkeepers, artisans who were rising in the social scale, and men who, helped by the energy given them by their new religion, had climbed by their own efforts. Free Trade was one of the issues which, by appealing to their self-interest, helped to buttress the Liberalism of their political thinking.

In addition to these semi-economic interests, there was at work in this period a political factor which issued in a silent revolution in English life. It had perhaps as much effect in shaping the course of middle-class political thought as any of the ancillary forces to be considered in a study of Methodism and Politics in the nineteenth century, and it supplied a reason and a direction for much of the political interest of Methodist laymen. The repeal of the Test and Corporation Acts in 1828 and the passing of the Municipal Corporations Act of 1835 had opened a new sphere of civic activity for business men. No more were Nonconformists liable to be shut out of politics by reason of their faith; nor were the local rulers of English towns to be elected, or co-opted, according to the obsolete and irrational methods of eighteenth-century politics. The triumph of Benthamite "Reason", which swept away the "Old Tories" at the general election in 1830, gave to England a system of local government which ensured that power should be in the hands of the middle classes.

These were the men whose influence in Methodism was becoming ever more important, and their feelings of self-importance in "Chapel Affairs" marched *pari passu* with their new sense of power in local politics. National questions only occasionally caused the Connexion trouble; local politics much more successfully wooed the ambitions of influential Methodists. The passing of the Reform Bill of 1832 had not involved any considerable change in the social composition of Parliament. Aristocrats continued in the main to represent industrial constituencies, but, in local affairs, the effects of the reforms began to be felt immediately.

At last the ice-age of English institutional and corporate life had come to an end, and the life of the community began to be remodelled according to the actual needs of the new economic society.[1]

Moreover that remodelling was being done by the community itself, and the first experiments in self-government were being worked out in municipal administration.

The functioning of local self-government was itself enough to foster democratic ideas, but there were other forces at work strengthening this tendency. The squire and the parson had, in the eighteenth century, held the reins of local power. Dissenting merchants had been subjected to various annoyances,[2] even where they had worked their way into affairs; but the events of 1835 changed the balance of power. When local government was to be based upon the suffrage of ratepayers, the middle classes were able to meet their old rivals on an equal footing. The power of wealth and numbers was theirs, and they ranged it against the prestige and tradition of their social superiors. The traditional rivalry between "Land" and "Trade", between "Church" and "Dissent", had found a new battle-ground in the council chambers of the reorganised municipalities, and at the polling booths of municipal elections.

Methodists had begun their independent ecclesiastical career as allies of the Established Church, but various exigencies of local politics ranged them more and more with the Dissenters. The rise of the High Church party increased Anglican arrogance towards Nonconformists,

[1] Trevelyan, *History of England*, p. 637.
[2] The most famous of these is the ruse by which the City of London paid for the Mansion House: by electing Dissenters to the office of Lord Mayor, and then fining them for their illegal holding of office.

and, although Methodists had been friendly towards Anglicanism, they began to find themselves despised by their former allies. Socially they were of the same class as the Dissenters, and common social and economic interests drew them closer together. Above all, like the Dissenters, they were unprivileged, and their friendliness to the Church did not serve to overcome that barrier. As self-made men, and as climbers in the social scale, many of them were particularly sensitive to the snobbery of the more aristocratic Tory Anglicans, who had only deigned to ally with them for electioneering purposes. Like most *nouveaux riches*, they were apt to set off their wealth and their "worth" against their neighbours' breeding and privilege. Their social "inferiority complex" made them apt to be hostile to social traditions which belonged peculiarly to their superiors, and to engender that feeling of general opposition to authority and tradition which is one of the bulwarks of political Liberalism. When this was linked with the social attraction between Nonconformist and Methodist laymen, whose interests so often coincided, it was not surprising that the Methodist laity, in spite of their ministers' opposition, were more and more drawn into the old Dissenting-Whig alliance, which still remained a powerful factor in the recruiting of the English Liberal party.[1]

A constant factor in contemporary politics was the issue of Disestablishment. It was an issue which, as directly as any in national affairs, appealed to the social

[1] It is significant that it has been in local politics, where personal and social reasons have always had more influence, that the Dissenting-Liberal alliance has longer retained its political vitality.

and ecclesiastical pride of the Methodist laity. They resented the arrogance of members of the Church of England who opposed them in Council meetings. They felt it inequitable that a Church which had failed to meet the needs of the growing populations of the northern towns should be left to enjoy wealth and privileges denied to the denomination which had carried out the work of evangelisation. Inspired, alike by denominational pride and by the utilitarianism of Bentham's searching question, "What is the use of it?" they turned the fire of their criticism against venerable absurdities, and against inequalities which only long usage had made tolerable, and they demanded an equalising of ecclesiastical positions. They found themselves increasingly in agreement with the Dissenters in their opposition to privilege in both Church and State; and, if Methodist ministers maintained the traditional conservative attitude which had prevented Disestablishment in 1832, Methodist laymen became as whole-hearted as their Dissenting brethren in their hostility to the exalted position of the Church of England. Local politics particularly encouraged such an alliance, for it was in local affairs that the grievances were most obvious, and in local affairs that there were so many other factors at work drawing Methodism towards Nonconformity.

So far as Methodism in this period was concerned, it may be said that, alongside its hatred and fear of Roman Catholicism, its attitude to the Church of England "as by law established" determined its policy in the controversies over Education, which were now becoming public issues. In what was held to be a religious rather

than a political question Methodist laymen resented concessions either to Anglicans or to Catholics. Whig misunderstanding of the Nonconformists' position delayed
the full development, but eventually it was not surprising
that on this question Methodists should ally themselves
with the party which had always leaned less towards the
Church, and which had unfurled the flag of " Liberty ".

Joseph Rayner Stephens has usually been considered
either as a Chartist agitator, or as a Tory opponent of that
triumph of Whig Utilitarianism, the Poor Law Amend-
ment Act. He was actually expelled from the Methodist
Connexion for his activities on behalf of a Church
Separation Society,[1] and his popularity in Lancashire
was due almost as much to his views on Disestablishment
as on social and economic questions. Within Methodism
discipline triumphed, and the trouble Stephens caused
was limited to south-east Lancashire; yet there were
many Methodist laymen who shared some of his views,
even when they accepted the ruling of Conference.
In any study of contemporary Methodism, Stephens and
his supporters are significant, not only as Chartists and
critics of the new Poor Law, but also as opponents of the
Establishment and of privilege. They called themselves
Tories, and they hated *laissez-faire*, but there were elements in their political creed which were of the stuff of
which nineteenth-century Liberalism was made.

If the Methodist laity was, in the second quarter of the
nineteenth century, politically influenced by social, economic, and political movements, it was also responsive
to the power of current ideas. The French Revolution

[1] Of which he was Secretary.

had frightened the English governing classes into a re-actionary, and not always intelligent conservatism, but the full exertion of their repressive powers did not serve to extinguish the flame which the Revolution had kindled in the minds of "the people". In the years which followed 1789 the Wesleyan Methodist Conference had not unsuccessfully combated the influence of French Revolutionary ideas upon the members of its own Societies; had it been the Inquisition itself, it could scarcely have succeeded in the era of the first Reform Bill.

Natural Rights, Individual Liberty, Democracy— based on the one and ensuring the other—these were the ideals which, to middle-class Methodists, seemed alike Liberal and scriptural. The attraction of the new thought had double force: in that it expressed the desires and ambitions, and appealed to the religious sentiments of the men from whose ranks were recruited both the new Liberal party and the new Methodist Church. They were men who were becoming, not so much class-conscious, as self-conscious. The fellowship in Methodism protected the Church against the worst dangers of class divisions; but its theology helped, in a peculiarly favourable age, to develop a strong individualistic self-consciousness, which led men to assert their rights in politics.[1] Believers in a doctrine of Assurance found much in the democratic ideals of Liberalism which might be regarded as a natural corollary to their religion. The results of this mental development were to be found both in political and in

[1] Compare S. G. Dimond, *Psychology of the Methodist Revival*, pp. 265–6: "Moreover spiritual illumination is individual, and while the matter of Methodist history may be social and moral, its form is individual and religious".

ecclesiastical matters, and the most obvious examples of a changed outlook were to be found in the disastrous period of the "Wesleyan Reform Agitation" of 1849 onwards.

The Industrial Revolution affected Methodism in a two-fold and divisive way. The self-control, thrift, and energy which attended the revival brought Methodists to the front in all the industrial advances. These also provoked a counter social and political revolution which was the dawn of the now dominant democracy. Behind the ecclesiastical divisions of Methodism lay that deep economic and political fissure.[1]

These political, economic, and ecclesiastical "fissures" were all the work of one upheaval, the upheaval which destroyed the "Wesleyan Reaction".

It was a vast complex of factors which overthrew the "Reaction", and an equally complicated development which produced the Methodist Liberal. Comparison of the two forces at work reveals a more than superficial connexion between them. The layman, anxious to assert his ecclesiastical rights against the paternal authority of his pastor, eager to mould his Church on a "New Testament model" which would ensure that there should be equality of power between the ministry and the laity, and ready even to pay the price of schism and exile to enforce the recognition of his rights, was a man who, as he forced his way into local politics, found himself at one with Dissenters in their attack on the Establishment, who, in national affairs, favoured Free Trade and hated

[1] Dr Scott Lidgett, "Presidential Address to the Uniting Conference", *The Times*, September 22nd, 1932.

"privilege", and who believed, especially in regard to the suffrage, in the democratic doctrines of the rights of man. His Liberalism and his zeal for a "Reformed" Methodism he regarded, not inaccurately, as two aspects of his religion. He had seized upon and developed the individualistic elements in the Revival, and he succeeded, before the end of the century, in carrying Methodism over into the ranks of Nonconformity. It was not John Wesley's Methodism which took this path, but a Methodism prepared by generations of unwitting gravitation towards Liberalism.

When Jabez Bunting's policy was confronted by a politically awakened laity, clashes were inevitable. The decisive trial of strength came in 1849; but that catastrophe was prefaced by a series of minor troubles, which testified to the existence of cross-currents beneath the seemingly placid surface of Methodist life. As "the Premier who never went out of office whoever might be President", as the director of Conference policy, and as the strictest of Methodist disciplinarians, Bunting usually impressed his will upon supporters or critics alike. But there were times when the strain proved too much for the centralised system of Methodism, when democrats refused to subordinate their principles to the smooth working of a policy with which they did not sympathise, and when the new wine of Liberal ideas burst the old wine-skins of rigid Connexionalism. All the conflicts which tore the nineteenth-century Methodist Church were struggles between authority and liberty, between the policy of Jabez Bunting and the democratic spirit of the "Liberal" section of the Church. It might almost be said that they were conflicts between an entrenched ministry and an ambitious laity. Personal quarrels aggravated grievances, but, beneath all personal differences, there was this clash of two opposing ideals. It is this which gives to the internal disruptions of the Connexion their significance in a study of the political life of Methodism, and which establishes the connexion between the break-up of the Reaction and the rise of the Methodist Liberal.

Bunting had, early in his career, flung himself against the irregularities of Revivalism,[1] and he had taken his part in freeing the Connexion from the embarrassments which some evangelists' methods had occasioned. But although the American evangelist, Caughey, caused considerable trouble in this period, and although many of the laity resented Bunting's treatment of him, it was not evangelistic excesses that divided the Church. The attack of the laity was directed against the basic principles of Bunting's policy, and against his autocratic supremacy within the Church. Men had been stimulated to question the fundamentals of the constitutions of both Church and State, and they were prepared if necessary to support their conclusions by revolution.

The "Leeds Organ Case" of 1827[2] was the result of a clash between Bunting, with his doctrine of pastoral authority, and the self-assertive Methodist laity of Yorkshire. The members of Brunswick Chapel, Leeds, ob-

[1] In 1806 he was concerned in the "Band Room Methodists" schism in Manchester. See *Life*, 1, 272–6, and, for a reasoned statement of his position, Appendix K, pp. 425–38.
[2] The organ installed at Brunswick Chapel, Leeds, it was said, cost "£1000 and 1000 members".

jected on "Protestant"[1] grounds to the installation of an organ, but they were lashed into resolute opposition by Bunting's high-handed and unconstitutional treatment of the question. The setting aside by Conference of the views of the Society and the decision of the District Meeting, and the trial of the malcontents by an unconstitutional Special District Meeting led to schism in the Leeds Circuit. It became more than a domestic brawl when that champion of Yorkshire Liberalism, and overt enemy of the conservatism of Wesleyan Methodism, *The Leeds Mercury*, seized the opportunity to make an attack upon the official policy, and publicly sided with the "Nonconformist Methodists".

By accepting this aid the Leeds malcontents laid themselves open to the charge made by their opponents that they were politically minded, and that the dispute was a thinly disguised "Radical" attempt to overthrow Methodism. The struggle was represented by the champions of Conference as one between the principles of Methodism and of Congregationalism, and the dissentients as rebels against pastoral authority. Whatever the truth of the charge, the latter imputation was soon made to square with the facts, and the Leeds agitators threw off the yoke of their ministers, and formed a small Nonconformist denomination of their own. Liberal preachers, opposed to their political associations, disavowed them, even when they had little sympathy with the treatment meted out to them by Conference. It was a lay movement, and the first concrete manifestation in the Methodism of the nine-

[1] The secessionists later called themselves "Protestant Methodists", or "Nonconformist Methodists".

teenth century of that grim insistence upon "rights" so characteristic of contemporary Liberals, and particularly of those with "Nonconformist Consciences". It was that spirit which alike divided and transformed Methodism.

The expulsion of Joseph Rayner Stephens in 1834 was accompanied within the Methodist Connexion by a semi-political crisis brought about by *The Christian Advocate*. This was the first of a series of "Liberal" newspapers which, by their outspoken criticism of Conference and its Conservatism, gave expression to the half-hidden ambitions of the laity. Conference succeeded in suppressing the obnoxious journal, but not before its circulation in many Methodist homes had sown seeds of revolt. *The Christian Advocate*, run by Stephens' brother and a few kindred spirits, was, like its successors, to have but a short life. *The Watchman's*[1] comment in 1849 in its notice of the first number of *The Wesleyan Times*,[2] that its own continued existence and the repeated failure of such papers as its latest contemporary bore witness to the real views of most Methodists, was not unjustified. The great mass of Methodist opinion was opposed to the mixing of politics with religion; but that papers such as these should have had a wide circulation amongst mem-

[1] *The Watchman* was a Methodist newspaper which strongly supported Dr Bunting and the Conference party. Begun in 1835, it came to be regarded almost as an official organ by 1849, but it was always run independently by laymen—as were all the Methodist newspapers. It was, in its political opinions, unashamedly Conservative, and the political news, like its rivals, published each week was always given with a strong Tory bias. See *passim*.

[2] *The Wesleyan Times*, like *The Christian Advocate*, was a paper started to give expression to the views of the "Liberal" opposition in Methodism.

bers of the Church reveals the existence of an opposition, which even the orthodoxy of *The Watchman* could not gainsay. They represented an effort on the part of a laity, shut out from Conference, to find expression for their hopes, and, under the cover of press anonymity, to spread the views of a minority, in a way which Conference discipline would have made impossible otherwise. They took up the pen when they could not make their voices heard.

The case of Warren's expulsion in 1835 involved the Wesleyan Methodist Church in an action which called in question its most characteristic ecclesiastical element—its Connexional system. Dr Warren, after bitterly attacking Bunting and the Theological Institution, over which it was intended that the latter should preside, had refused to account for his behaviour to the Conference, which, he held, was a court sympathetic to his opponent. He was expelled for contumacy, but he refused to accept the sentence of a court whose validity he had called in question by his whole course of conduct. He was, at the time, stationed in Manchester, and he brought a Chancery action against the Wesleyan Methodist Conference, claiming the right, despite his expulsion, to continue as minister of the Oldham Street Chapel there.

The future of Wesley's Connexional system depended upon the result of the action. Had Warren won his case, any malcontent minister might have taken the decision as establishing a precedent for turning his Circuit into a Congregationalist "charge". The judgment of the Vice-Chancellor[1] was upheld on appeal to the Lord Chancellor Lyndhurst; and the right of jurisdiction

[1] See reports of the case in Hobill Collection under "Warrenite Controversy".

over all Methodist Societies and their pastors was given to Conference by the highest legal authorities. The decision established the Connexional system. The "Warren Case" had been a test case. No minister expelled by Conference ever again appealed to the Law Courts against his sentence. The system of Methodism had been saved from the dangers that were threatening it from those within its ranks who were attracted by Congregationalist models, and who valued their own rights above the integrity of the Connexion.

There were, however, other results of the agitation. The Wesleyan Connexional system had been saved, but there were many sympathisers with Warren and his ideas who were ready to leave the "old body" to vindicate their position. These men found, in Samuel Warren and Robert Eckett, two leaders who were ready to organise a "Wesleyan Methodist Association" to embody the ideals of the "Warrenites". By 1839 the movement had 28,000 members and 600 chapels.[1] A movement of such a size was patently more than an obscurantist protest against an educated ministry; it showed the two usual features of Methodist dissensions in the nineteenth century—personal and ecclesiastical. The two leaders represented the two sides of the dispute, and their different characters fitted each to play his part.

Warren disliked the hegemony of Bunting in the Wesleyan Connexion, but, although he had helped to set them forth, he would not accept the principles of government adopted by the Association.[2] Eckett's quarrel with

[1] About 8000 originally seceded in 1835, but the Protestant and Arminian Methodists joined them in 1836.
[2] He later became an Anglican clergyman.

the Connexion was the result of his views on Church government and laymen's rights. Warren represented the personal aspect of the dispute; Eckett the theoretical. The former, in this case as usual, occasioned the hostilities; the latter developed the clash into a schism.

Robert Eckett was a Methodist of the new school. He was a Yorkshireman who had made a fortune as a builder in London before he gave his services to the ministry of the Association. In spirit he never ceased to be a layman, and his aim in life was to vindicate laymen's rights in Methodism. The Methodist New Connexion held out its friendship to the Association, but the negotiations for union came to nothing, because Eckett insisted upon there being left to each Circuit free choice of either a minister or a layman as its representative to Conference, whereas the system of the New Connexion ensured, within the Conference, an equal representation of each order. Within the Association, there was secured to the Societies which had seceded a larger measure of Circuit independence than the New Connexion was prepared to allow. Influenced by Congregationalist ideals, Eckett looked to the societies represented in Conference; the Methodist New Connexion, true to its Methodist antecedents, regarded the representatives of the Circuits as members of a larger whole. The negotiations for union were not to be successful until 1907. The new body, in accord with Eckett's ideas, was to be a "Wesleyan Methodist Association" rather than a Wesleyan Methodist Connexion.

Such Liberal and Independent elements were to be expected in a plan formed by men like this bourgeois

Yorkshireman and like John Petrie, coadjutor of Bright and Cobden in the Corn Law and Church Rate controversies, and leader of the Rochdale "Petitioners". As men who, by their own efforts and their established "worth", had risen to a position of local influence and eminence, and as men who found in the New Testament the apology for their political faith and their ecclesiastical ideals, they were drawn to the most democratic of all Church constitutions, that of Congregationalism. The Methodism which had been responsible for their conversion held their affections, but they themselves worked in it a revolution. From men such as Eckett came the leadership in that Methodist revolution.

In estimating the Liberal opposition to the "Conference party", the opposition in Conference itself ought not to be overlooked. It was weak, and continually browbeaten by Dr Bunting, but the great man's stronghold was not filled entirely by his satellites. Daniel Isaac, Thomas Galland, Joseph Fowler, Dr Beaumont, all at some time led the opposition to Jabez Bunting, and, by both sides, they were characterised as the "Liberal section of Conference".[1] In politics, their respect for the standard of "Liberty" rather than that of "Authority" made them, not Radicals, but, like all the leaders of Methodist reform movements from Kilham to Griffith, Liberals, whose attacks upon Bunting's clericalism and upon political inequalities in national affairs were both manifestations of the same spirit. Their attitude was perhaps best summed up by one of them, Galland, when he said: "I dread extremes; but the extreme of Radical-

[1] See *Sidelights*, *passim*, on this.

159

ism is worse than the extreme of Conservatism".[1] However Liberal such men might be, they would never be likely to allow social theories to sweep them into Socialism, for their Liberalism was almost as much a bulwark against that as against Paternalism.

This clerical Liberalism was the fruit of different seeds from those from which sprang much of the layman's political creed, but both the type itself and the factors producing it are of importance in a study of Liberalism in Methodism. These Liberal preachers supplied the leaders in ecclesiastical disputes, and their views were always treated with respect. Through them many of the "theological" ideas in the nineteenth-century Liberal creed came to exercise influence upon the thought of their flocks. The ministry and the laity were continually interacting upon one another's ideas, and, if laymen were often more liberal than their pastors, men like Isaac and Galland helped to develop the thinking of the newly enfranchised classes who filled their churches.

The ministry was recruited from the Societies, and therefore it derived from the same social strata as did the Church as a whole. It was affected by all the social forces which affected the Church in the new age, and this at a time when many of the traditions of the Reaction had been weakened by the passage of time. Men brought up in surroundings where Radicalism and the French Revolutionary doctrines of Liberty, Equality, and Fraternity flourished, ignorant of the historical basis of the Connexional scheme, and attracted by ideas of ecclesiastical and political liberty, were entering the Methodist

[1] *Sidelights*, p. 571.

ministry and contributing their quota to the work of destroying the "Wesleyan Reaction". To them Bunting's autocracy and his conservatism seemed, not expressions of a traditional attitude, but obscurantist attempts to usurp a power vested truly in "the people". As in the case of Kilham, their thinking may have been unhistoric, but it was symptomatic of the change which had come about in Methodism.

There were also men in the ministry whose Dissenting origins predisposed them to friendship with Nonconformity. The influence of Presbyterianism upon the Methodist New Connexion movement has been noticed.[1] In the controversies of the mid-nineteenth century the chief Nonconformist influence was Congregational rather than Presbyterian. The Wesleyan Methodist Association of 1835, and the Wesleyan Methodist Reform Union, which was produced by the 1849 disturbance, were both deeply tinctured with Congregationalism. They owed some of their inspiration in this respect both to their local contacts with the Independents in the north of England, and to the Dissenters who, from the first, had found a place within Methodism. With them, reaction against Anglo-Catholicism did not coexist with a "Stock Still" policy of friendship with or admiration of the Church of England. They were the people most anxious that Methodism should take its place in English life as the largest and most important of the Free Churches, and they were the people most open to the influence of the Dissenting-Whig alliance.

Connected with this was a theological movement, of

---

[1] *Vide supra*, pp. 83–4.

which the exponent was Daniel Isaac. His book, *An Investigation of Ecclesiastical Claims*, was condemned by the Methodist Conference.[1] It was a thorough-going onslaught upon all ecclesiastical claims, and, although its violence shocked Conference, it expressed the opinions of many Methodists, and especially of laymen from the manufacturing districts of the north—always the most fertile soil for revolutionary seeds. Isaac attacked all doctrines of a special call to the ministry as minimising the great Christian truth of the Priesthood of All Believers, and, from this, he drew the corollary that divine authority belonged, not to the separated ministry, but to the whole Church:

> The exclusive power claimed by priests of adding to their own body must be given up, and the right of the laity to assume or confer the holy office must be granted.[2]

Although Daniel Isaac's book never achieved wide circulation, it had significance as a sample of the complete Protestantism professed by some of the "Liberals". The publication of a book might be forbidden; the propagation of such ideas could not be checked. They had their part in directing the thinking, both ecclesiastical and political, of contemporary Methodists, and they swelled the rising tide of Liberalism.

Jabez Bunting and his party in Conference successfully kept down the opposition there, but their chance came to the minority after Bunting's death. Seeds which had

[1] The censure passed upon the book by Conference was printed in the *Minutes* and circulated throughout the Connexion. The Book Room refused to publish the *Investigation*.

[2] Quoted in *Life of Bunting*, II, 105.

been slow in germinating then sprang into flower. Never again was there to be in Methodism so powerful a Conservative force, never again such a regimentation of thought and practice as that which had existed during the "Pontificate". The Liberals, both lay and clerical, were able to go forward with their work of turning Methodism into a great Liberal Nonconformist Church. By the time of Hugh Price Hughes, and the formation of the Free Church Council, the unsuspected revolution had been carried through. In Bunting's day the Liberals in Methodism had been a troublesome minority; at the close of the nineteenth century they included in their ranks the leaders of the Church, whether in Conference, in the pulpit, or on public platforms. Galland and Isaac, Fowler and Beaumont, were the precursors of a great body of "clerical" Liberals. If the development was slow, it must be remembered that Bunting's position in Conference was almost unassailable, that ancillary factors, such as economic considerations, whilst affecting lay sentiment, carried comparatively little weight with men in the ministry, and that the anti-clericalism of Liberalism struck at the power of the Methodist preacher. This last factor naturally stiffened the resistance to change of a purely clerical body such as Conference.

Methodism, in the years between 1827 and 1846, contained a multitude of ideas and fashions of thought which were shaping the minds of its members. Laymen especially were susceptible to their influence; for, not only were laymen in Methodism generally ignorant of the historical reasons for Methodism's paternal government, but many of those who were becoming members were from the class most open to the appeal of current Liberalism. Tradition received scant respect from men concerned to win their "rights", and such men eagerly accepted suggestions that privileges, whether in Church or State, should be subjected to rigorous examination.

The germination of Liberal ideas was a subconscious process; the people most affected by the movement were oblivious of its extent. But what had previously been implicit became explicit in the controversies provoked by Jabez Bunting's autocracy. The quarrels usually began because of personal grievances; they always issued in the enunciation of principles of Church government, which the necessities of conflict clarified. By 1849 the issue had been stated as one between a clerical "tyranny" and a democracy. The "Regulations of 1835", by which the Superintendent was declared to be sole judge of the sentence to be passed upon an offending member, because such power was "essential to the scriptural duties and functions of the pastoral office",[1] provoked the hostility and resolute opposition of the democrats, and they revealed the specific difficulties which Democracy was bound to encounter in any clash with Conference orthodoxy. That clash, when it came in 1849, destroyed the "Reaction".

[1] *Minutes of Conference of* 1835, quoted Peirce, pp. 67–74. These regulations roused much hostility amongst the malcontents of 1849.

CHAPTER VII

THE "WESLEYAN REACTION" BREAKS UP: THE "WESLEYAN REFORM" AGITATION, 1846–51

The year 1849 stands as a landmark in Methodist history. Beside the disruption of that year all the previous disturbances in Methodism rank as insignificant. In 1849, not only did the Connexion lose more members than it had lost in all the previous secessions put together, but it was shaken to its foundations in every part of the country. The policy of Jabez Bunting had, by virtue of an efficient Connexionalism, been carried into effect throughout Methodism, and the authority of the collective pastorate had been established from Shetland to Penzance. The influence of Liberal ideas had been wellnigh as extensive, and, especially in the great industrial districts of the north and midlands, there had grown up an unorganised but Connexion-wide sentiment of opposition to clerical claims. In 1849 the two forces were launched, the one against the other, and in almost every Circuit of Methodism the resultant impact was felt. In the trial of strength between the two great nineteenth-century developments in Wesleyan Methodism, the "Wesleyan Reaction" finally broke up. There was left, in its place, a divided Church, which had moved far from the position of its founder.

In this great struggle, the man who had, almost throughout the century, guided the policy of the Church, played comparatively little part. He was growing old, and his power as a public speaker was sensibly weakening.[1] He left the burden of the battle to be borne by his supporters and disciples, and men like George Osborn showed the same ruthless vigour as that which had characterised their leader in the days of his greatest power. The "Liberals" also had found fresh leaders. Beaumont still took part, but at the centre of the conflict were Everett, Dunn, and Griffith, three ministers who only achieved Connexional fame in the 'forties. To them the minority looked for direction, and to them it gave its sympathy and allegiance, when they were expelled by Conference in 1849.

Yet if the two sides had new leaders they had still the old policies. Centralisation and pastoral supremacy were the chief planks in the "Conference party" platform; "Liberty" and lay representation those upon which the minority stood. Dr Bunting was personally implicated by the attacks upon him and upon his policy, but the struggle against Osborn's "Declaration"[2] revealed the theoretical side of the conflict. It was, on a larger scale, a part of the same struggle which had been manifest in 1797, in 1827, and in 1835—the struggle between the forces of authority and the forces of liberty within the Methodist Church. There were ministers and laymen on both sides, but it would be largely true to say that this conflict between the conservative and the reforming forces in Methodism was one between a clerical party and a lay party. Neither fully represented the transformed character of the Church; each represented an essential element in it. The rigidifying of Church organisation had

[1] *Sidelights*, pp. 281–2.   [2] *Vide infra*, pp. 172–6.

left the adjustment of relations between these two elements to the arbitrament of force. The clash between them cost the Wesleyan Methodist Church 100,469 members in five years.[1]

The discontent within the Connexion had been revealed by the publication of the notorious *Fly Sheets*,[2] and by the war of pamphlets and papers which had followed their appearance. This encounter between the pamphleteers on either side, carried on behind the shield of anonymity, was, without doubt, the most lamentable episode in Methodist history. Both sides, casting away Christian charity, indulged in unscrupulous misrepresentation and insinuation. The champions of either side were unworthy of their causes; but the principles for which they fought were of more permanent value than the squibs they wrote to advocate them. The *Fly Sheets* on the one side, and *Papers on Wesleyan Matters* on the other (to mention the two most famous), are no longer read, but the new Methodist Church, achieved by the Union of 1932, has found a place in its polity for ideas which both sets of controversialists so shamelessly caricatured.

It has been pleaded by one party, in extenuation of such methods, that only anonymity could have protected the Liberal section from persecution by the governing majority in Conference;[3] and, by the other side, that the *Fly Sheets*, by their violence, provoked a righteous indignation, which issued in equally violent replies. It may also be contended that these mutual recriminations served, by their very exaggerations, to bring to a head

[1] *Sidelights*, p. 494.
[2] The first two numbers appeared in 1846, the third in 1847, and the fourth (and last) in 1848.
[3] See Chew, *James Everett*, pp. 373–9.

167

poisons within the system of Methodism. Both sides were driven into making extreme assertions regarding their position, and, in the event, moderate men, disgusted by so sordid a controversy, were able to see the dangers besetting the path of either wing. When the excitement had died down it was possible for them to take control and to steer the middle course which alone could avoid both sides' difficulties.

Such a contention is strengthened by the fact that both sides in the controversy represented parties within Methodism, and that, as each provoked the excesses of the other, both were struggling for mastery in the counsels of the Church. It is also true that, after the "bloodletting" of 1849, Wesleyan Methodism gradually became more liberal, both ecclesiastically and politically.[1] It may have needed the excesses of its "Paper war" to make the Methodist Conference realise that there was developing a dangerous cleavage between a Conservative and authoritarian ministry and a Liberal and democratic laity, which was prepared to fight for its new-born ideals against either tradition or oppression.

The *Fly Sheets*, published "By order of the Corresponding Committee for detecting, exposing and correcting abuses. London, Manchester, Bristol, Liverpool, Birmingham, Leeds, Hull, Glasgow",[2] were

[1] Lay representation in Conference was conceded in 1877, and the concession actualised in 1878.

[2] This list of towns may have been added to render more difficult the work of detection, but it also reveals the centres in which the authors believed their supporters to be. They were places in which middle-class Liberals were likely to be strong, both in numbers and in influence in the Church.

concerned with the need for Connexional reforms. Their onslaughts upon Bunting and the Metropolitan Committees, upon the "master mind" and his "located, centralised clique",[1] were intended to issue in concrete proposals for democratising Connexional government. Their coarse personal imputations were, in part, expressions of personal hostility to Bunting, and, in part, attacks upon the system he had built up. These anonymous pamphlets were originally sent to ministers only, but, in the heat of the controversy, they were scattered broadcast throughout the Connexion.

Their influence, like that of the counter-pamphlets, *Papers on Wesleyan Matters*[2] and *Vates*, was generally restricted to clerical circles, but the laity, whose opinions they had expressed, were fed by newspapers representing the two sides to the controversy. It is these newspapers which reveal the connexion between the ecclesiastical and the political sides to the Reformers' hopes.

The Watchman[3] became, during this period, the chief organ of defence for the Conference party, and it admitted to its columns correspondence of a most violent character.[4] *The Wesleyan Times*[5] was the Liberal champion, and

[1] F.S. No. 1, p. 19.
[2] First published January 1st, 1849.
[3] Started January 1835.
[4] See *passim* for the years 1849 onwards.
[5] Begun January 8th, 1849. It was the most successful paper the Liberal Methodists ever ran, and it had a longer and more vigorous life than any of its predecessors. Its editorial descendants were *The Free Methodist* and, after the Union of 1907, *The United Methodist*. Since the Union of 1932 *The United Methodist* has amalgamated with *The Methodist Recorder*, the descendant of *The Watchman*. Such a fusion of old enemies bears witness to the deadness of the controversies which called forth their first rivalry.

through these two papers the Methodist layman's sympathies were roused by either side into partisan enthusiasm. These newspapers, for they were more than mere denominational chronicles, found their way into many a home in Methodism, and each sowed seeds of dissension and bitterness there.

In addition, they both helped to shape the political thinking of Methodists upon subjects of national interest. Alongside their denominational polemics they printed general news (both home and foreign), stock exchange prices (for the benefit of their middle-class patrons), and political news and views. Parliamentary debates challenged sermons for space, and "leaders" on government policy were constant features in both papers. Amongst the lower-middle and working classes, which formed the main strength of Methodism, there was not, before 1851, that tradition of reading *The Times* or *The Daily News*, which was a common feature in the lives of many of the wealthy Nonconformist families,[1] and in many working class and lower-middle class homes, where they were the only newspapers taken, their political views, as well as their ecclesiastical, must have received the attention and respect of their readers. They exercised the power of the press over the minds of the very classes which were becoming interested in matters of national policy, and they supplied the spectacles through which those men looked out upon affairs of Church and State.

The publication of political news and commentary was undertaken without scrupulous adherence to the "No Politics Rule". Papers which were unofficial, and which

[1] See J. L. Garvin, *Life of Joseph Chamberlain*.

were financed by laymen, could not be brought under Conference discipline to the same extent as could ministerial writings. They were free to take party sides, and they both did so. Moreover, they took the sides that might be expected from a knowledge of their ecclesiastical views: *The Watchman* the Conservative, and *The Wesleyan Times* the Liberal. To take but one example amongst many. On matters of fiscal policy, which were exciting great public interest at the time of the Corn Law agitation, *The Watchman* expressed its distrust of the value of Mr Cobden's work, and it had nothing but hostility for his appeals to "the people" and for the democratic and "anti-privilege" attitude of his supporters in the north of England. *The Wesleyan Times*, on the other hand, gave Bright and Cobden its whole-hearted support, hailed Free Trade as the restoration to Englishmen of unjustly filched rights, and appealed to the bourgeoisie and working classes against the antiquated privilege of the aristocracy and the House of Lords.[1]

The Watchman was careful to publish its loyalty to the British Constitution and to its guardians—the Crown, Lords and Commons. It had, towards the Constitution, that complacent attitude which represents much of the strength of British Conservatism, and which rightly belongs to Toryism rather than to Whiggism.[2] *The Wes-*

[1] A reading of the files of these newspapers reveals the fact that on almost all subjects of political, as of ecclesiastical import, *The Watchman* was Conservative and *The Wesleyan Times* Liberal. The significance of the Free Trade alignment comes from this.

[2] That the Whigs have at times (e.g. after 1688 and again after 1832) been as complacent in their attitude to the Constitution as their rivals is undeniable; but if the Whigs be taken as the champions of "Liberty", e.g. as expressed in a "Constitutional"

leyan Times paid no obsequious attentions to the perfect plan even of 1832. It represented a section of the community which was still dissatisfied with the extent of the franchise, and which regarded the Reform Bill of 1832 as but the first step towards the attainment of manhood suffrage. It encouraged the ambitions of the politically dissatisfied classes in England, and, in its leading articles, championed the cause of the working man, "oppressed" by the privileges of an idle aristocracy. It advocated "Free Trade" as a means of sweeping away obsolete abuses, and of freeing the energies of men to develop their own special gifts. Against Tory respect for institutions, it raised the Individualist standard, and the Liberal war cry of *laissez-faire*. In a word, the organ of the "Conference party" expressed the traditional Wesleyan Conservatism which, albeit unofficially, had already exerted considerable force in English politics; the paper whose primary object was to advocate reforms in Methodist government acted as the mouthpiece of the more recently developed Liberal minority in Methodism.

The Conference of 1849 was held in Manchester in the midst of great excitement. The pamphlet and newspaper controversy begun in 1846 had produced an electric atmosphere that portended a storm, and the storm burst with devastating violence during the meetings of Con-

Government safeguarding the liberties of the subject, and the Tories as the champions of "Authority", e.g. as expressed in strong or paternal government, it may with justice be held that a satisfaction with the powers that be comes more *naturally* to Tories than to Whigs. Whig enthusiasm for the English Constitution has usually been the fruit of a belief that the liberties of the subject had been secured by minimising governmental interference, or by securing its control by "the People".

ference. The bitter spirit shown in the apologetics of both
sides had been intensified by the "Test" instituted by
Osborn, Chettle, and Hargreaves—three of the most
ardent of Bunting's admirers. They had attempted to
make a voluntary declaration denying authorship of the
obnoxious pamphlets into a test of the loyalty of all
Methodist ministers. Conference had "permitted"
them to circulate the declaration in 1847;[1] but, to make
signing it a necessary condition for withdrawing suspicion of complicity, was to overstep the bounds of that
permission. Letters, hinting that non-subscribers would
be treated as suspects when the method of the "brotherly
question" was put into practice at the next Conference,
were sent out to quicken the zeal of those whose signatures
were not immediately forthcoming. Every effort was
made to ensure the narrowing down of suspicion to those
who would not sign. The methods used frightened many
a liberal-minded minister who disliked the procedure,
into signing the declaration in order to clear himself from
suspicion. Men who, like Fowler, could not conscien-
tiously "denounce the *Fly Sheets* as wicked lies because
many of the sentiments therein had been theirs for
years", were left to choose between subscription to a
test they hated, and the unjust suspicion of men they
loved. Most of them chose subscription as the lesser evil.

If some had been frightened into compliance with the
wishes of the dominant party, there were several prominent members of Conference who could not be intimidated
in that way, and whose opposition to the declaration was

[1] Harrison, *Companion to the Minutes of the Conference of* 1849,
pp. 70–1.

stiffened by the efforts of its champions. These men went to Manchester determined to fight for the privileges of Englishmen, and resolved to resist the inquisitorial methods of the governing clique. Beaumont and Fowler hated the excesses of the *Fly Sheets*, but they refused to sign Osborn's "Declaration", which they regarded as illiberal and as *ultra vires*. That they would be in a minority was certain; but they went to Conference in a militant spirit. The "government" was determined to "cast out the scorner" by whatever means, and the Liberal minority was equally resolved to resist any autocratic action on the part of the bureaucracy it had grown to distrust. In such circumstances it was impossible that the 1849 Conference could be anything but a stormy one. The controversies of the last three years had produced too dangerous an "Ultraism" on both sides to make a peaceful settlement of Methodist differences likely.

A study of the politics of Methodism does not require a detailed description of the events of this Conference, but there were certain incidents in connexion with the expulsion "for contumacy"[1] of Everett, Dunn, and Griffith that had repercussions in every department of Methodism, and that gave to the "Liberals" a dangerous weapon of attack. As revealing the ideas of government held by either side, they have great importance in a study of the political alliances forming within Methodism.

The suspicions of the majority had fastened themselves on Messrs Everett, Dunn, and Griffith, who were men uncompromisingly opposed to the power of the Metro-

[1] See the Conference letter on the expulsions—Harrison, pp. 141–8.

politan Committees, and who were suspected of implica-
tion in publishing the *Fly Sheets*. Round them the
proceedings of Conference moved.[1] Above all, the suspicions of the Conference party had fallen upon James
Everett, who had previously been convicted of similar (if
less obnoxious) activities,[2] and whose scant respect for
the rules of the Connexion was shown by the fact that,
in spite of Wesley's ruling of 1768,[3] he ran a book-shop
in Manchester (under an assumed name). Moreover, the
sarcastic and derogatory tone of the *Fly Sheets* had well-
known parallels in the style of his other published works.
It has never been conclusively proved that Everett wrote
the *Fly Sheets*, but circumstantial evidence is strong
against him. They were the characteristic work of a man
such as he was.

Appealing to the letter of the law, and to what he held
to be the spirit of the "brotherly question"—the method
which Conference had resolved to adopt in the investigation of the case—Everett refused either to sign the
"Declaration", to give a direct answer to the question of
his complicity, or to admit the right of Conference to

[1] There are more materials concerning this Conference than
concerning any other in Methodist history. In addition to the usual
authorities, *Minutes* and *Sidelights*, there were reports in denominational papers and (most useful of all) a *Companion to the Minutes of
the Conference of* 1849 prepared by the Rev. Samuel Harrison, with
full reports of the debates. There are also many references in the
biographies of the men who took part in the struggles of that year.

[2] His *Wesleyan Takings or Centenary Sketches* (originally published anonymously) had caused bitter feeling amongst many
ministers. The style of this book, as of the *Fly Sheets*, is full of
criticism of natural deficiencies and imputations of low motives.
Neither is the sort of book usually associated with the expressed
views of a minister upon his brethren! [3] *Vide supra*, p. 60 n.

enforce any such answer, especially when he was not given the name of his accuser.[1] Conference referred the matter to a Committee of Ex-Presidents, but added to it three Manchester Superintendents (including Osborn) who "had been painfully mixed up with the affair from the beginning".[2] The expulsion of Everett on the recommendation of this committee bore, in spite of Osborn's apologia, a dangerous resemblance to a party triumph over a troublesome opponent. Everett, quite impenitent, announced that his expulsion had been pre-determined by "the clique".

Excitement reached fever heat on the question of the reporting of Conference debates. Samuel Dunn, who had edited *The Wesley Banner*, a religious rather than an ecclesiastico-political paper, and William Griffith, who was taking notes for *The Wesleyan Times*, were arraigned on this question, and the subsequent proceedings of Conference revealed the temper of both sides. In a tempestuous scene, Dunn refused to answer the direct question of the President concerning the authorship of the *Fly Sheets*, unless he were allowed to explain his position of hostility to Osborn's "Declaration", which he characterised as "a measure that savoured more of Rome than of England, of Popery than of Methodism".[3] He also refused to give an undertaking to suppress *The Wesley Banner* or to cease reporting for *The Wesleyan Times*. His case was referred to the same committee as had dealt with Everett.

[1] Harrison, pp. 89–90.
[2] Beaumont had stigmatised Osborn as "Accuser of the Brethren". See Osborn's speech in his own defence, Harrison, pp. 97–9.
[3] See Harrison, pp. 110–11.

Dunn's trial respecting his connexion with *The Wes-leyan Times* was linked with that of William Griffith, who had refused to give an undertaking not to report for *The Wesleyan Times*, unless other members of Conference gave a similar undertaking concerning *The Watchman*.[1] Conference refused to allow Griffith to link the two questions of reporting to *The Watchman* and to its rival. Following Dr Bunting, who said:

It is a wrong done to *The Watchman* to put it into the same category as *The Wesleyan Times*. The general tone of the former is conservative of Methodism, but the latter is hostile to Methodism,[2]

it passed a resolution thanking *The Watchman* for its services, and condemning *The Wesleyan Times* and any who contributed thereto.

Dunn and Griffith counter-attacked, and, for their "contumacy", were both expelled. These three expulsions were to cost the Methodist Church dear. From their "unjust" treatment by Conference, the "Three Expelled" appealed to the public, and the circumstances of their trials lent strength to their case. On the question of reporting, it was not difficult, in the light of *The Watchman's* unscrupulous campaign against Fowler's candidature for the presidency in 1849, to convince the public of the justice of Atherton's outburst:

Well, have I then lived to learn that slander and detraction and unprovoked, ill-natured untruth are only wrong when resorted to by the opposite side?[3]

[1] Harrison, pp. 106–8.   [2] *Ibid.* p. 102.
[3] *Sidelights*, p. 441. Atherton was the father of the Liberal Attorney-General in 1861.

Whatever the rights or wrongs of the case in 1849, many of the actions of Conference, by their arrogant irresponsibility, had weakened its case in the eyes of the public.

From the sentence of Conference there was no legal right of appeal. The failure of Dr Warren's appeal to the Civil courts against his expulsion in 1835 had established the sovereign right of Conference to enforce discipline within the Connexion.[1] Everett, Dunn, and Griffith had no chance of constitutional redress. They felt themselves wronged and unjustly treated; but their wrongs could only be repaired by the action of the body which had committed them. The only other course open to them was one of agitation and of an appeal to the public. This course they took, and a struggle which had previously been waged in pamphlets, in the Methodist press, and in Conference, found a new battle-ground on public platforms throughout the country.

The "Three Expelled", as they called themselves, carried their appeal from "Conference justice" to general equity, from the decision of a clerical bureaucracy to the sympathy of the "Man in the Pew". "Giant Meetings", beginning with one at Exeter Hall,[2] were addressed by the three leaders of the movement, who described their wrongs, and received the sympathy and help of their lay supporters. Men whose equalitarian principles had been kept below the surface by their love for their ministers, were roused to a passionate denunciation of clerical autocracy. Posing as the champions of laymen's rights, Everett, Dunn, and Griffith warned their large and ex-

---

[1] *Vide supra*, pp. 156–7.
[2] August 31st, 1849. See reports in *The Wesleyan Times*.

citable audiences that the rule of the "Platform" in Conference spelt the destruction of lay privileges, and the stultification of all attempts at Liberal reform. Throughout the country they went, sowing seeds of discontent and of hostility to the "government", and it was in the great industrial centres of Methodism that they drew their largest and most enthusiastic audiences. They chose large towns for their campaign, and found there, not only greater numbers of supporters than elsewhere, but men whose whole attitude to life disposed them to agree with the arguments that they used against ministerial tyranny and the restriction of laymen's rights and functions in the Church.

Their quarrel at first was with a party in Methodism rather than with Methodism itself. They directed their arguments against abuses in the administration of the Connexion,[1] and demanded sweeping reforms therein. Their first meetings were for Methodists, and, both by word and action, they advertised the fact that, although they had been expelled by Conference, they intended to conduct a campaign of reform *within* the Church. Their appeal to the general public was for support; their appeal to Methodist laymen a call to work with them for much-needed reforms. They believed that their expulsion had been a manifestation of the anti-Liberal spirit, which had, so far, successfully withheld from the laity such participation in Connexional government as was theirs in their own right, and they put themselves at the head of a

[1] In doing this they were carrying on the policy of the *Fly Sheets*, which had levelled criticism not against Methodism but against its leaders.

reforming party. They hoped that, so organised, the laity might be able to bring sufficient pressure to bear upon Conference to compel consideration of their claims.

Like all reformers, they maintained that they were but trying to restore the purity of the old forms, and part of their attack upon "Conference Methodism" was made as professed "children of John Wesley". They believed that the reforms they advocated were necessary if true Methodism was to survive, for they put no trust in the type which was represented by the Conference. If it be true that these reformers were "men who did not understand growth and development, and knew no progress but that which involved destruction and revolution",[1] it is also true that they believed that such measures as they had been driven to advocate were necessary to restore John Wesley's ideals to his Church. Like Kilham, they accepted, as necessary, the paternalism of Wesley, but like him also, they believed that the time had come for the Church to develop the latent democracy they saw in Wesley's system. They believed that the rule of Bunting and the "Directory" was stifling those Liberal elements of equality, and of freedom of speech and expression of opinion, which, as integral parts of Methodism, were essential to its well-being.

Their agitation for internal reform led to violent Connexional disturbances. Meetings, held on Trust premises in defiance of Superintendents' prohibitions, led to expulsions. Stormy debates between the two parties in Circuit meetings issued in secessions of discontented laymen who resented the attitude of their ministers. Cries

[1] *Life of Bunting*, II, 348.

of "Stop the Supplies!" to enforce redress of grievances added to the excitement. The Conferences of 1850 and 1851 determined to adopt a strong policy, and, as the Conference of 1849 had cast out the ringleaders, to root out discontent in every part of the Connexion. Circuit memorials, referring to the cases of 1849, were arrogantly ignored, and their signatories lectured by Superintendents on the duties of obeying the powers that be. "Die-Hards", with the support of Bunting, announced that, though the process cost 30,000 members, yet would they restore peace to the Connexion.[1] Three times that number was the price they paid for the "success" of their policy. "Ubi solitudinem faciunt pacem appellant." The "law of 1835", whereby members might be expelled according to the decision of the Superintendent alone, led to wholesale expulsions wherever an autocratic minister encountered reforming laymen.[2]

A movement which had begun by desiring domestic reform was forced by circumstances to organise itself as a separate body, whose "Delegate Meetings" grew into the "Conference of the People" as opposed to the "Conference of Priests".[3] Not till 1857 was the decisive step taken, but in that year, by a union with the "Wesleyan Methodist Association", and an unqualified acceptance

[1] *Sidelights*, p. 474.
[2] This "law" had been enacted by Conference at the time of the Warrenite disturbances, and had involved a modification of the "Plan of Pacification" of 1797. It was a law to regulate the relations between Superintendent Ministers and the Circuit Committees it set up for specific purposes. See *Minutes* for 1835.
[3] At the Delegate Meeting at Sheffield in 1852 there were reported to be 47,598 members and 1481 chapels in sympathy with the Reformers. Chew, *James Everett*, p. 437.

of its Deed Poll, the "United Methodist Free Churches" were formed to rival the old Connexion. The final result of the appeal to the public had been the setting up of a new Methodist Church, with its chief strength in the industrial north and midlands, and with a constitution more democratic and more Nonconformist than that of its Mother Church. It was the greatest, as it had been the most violent, of all the manifestations of the new Liberal spirit abroad in Methodism. Everett, Dunn, and Griffith were its prophets and "martyrs"; the United Methodist Free Churches and their constitution its expression.

The dual nature of the aggrieved ministers' appeal for internal reform and for outside sympathy should not obscure the all-important fact that, in either case, that appeal contained the same elements. They addressed their audiences as Englishmen whose liberties were sacred. The Liberal arguments which had coloured their writings and characterised their newspapers, fired their eloquence, and gave to them words which would not have sounded unfamiliar from the lips of Bright and Cobden. The "Three Expelled" were all Liberals in politics, as were most of their supporters, and that political faith was a natural corollary to the ecclesiastical and theological ideals they had set before themselves.

Appealing from the "Law of the Minutes" to the "Law of Christ", they maintained that

The People only claim what Christ as the Head of the Church has given them; the Preachers are resolved to keep all that their Minutes assign to them.[1]

[1] Chew, *Life and Letters of William Griffith*, p. 85.

In the name of the "Priesthood of All Believers", which has always been the basic doctrine of Nonconformist Democracy, they denounced the clerical autocracy of the men who had

never cared to be *with* the people; but...careful to be, according to [their] judgement, *for* them.[1]

With such beliefs, it was but natural that they should gather to their side the men to whom contemporary democratic ideas were proving so attractive, the men who, for more than economic reasons, were supporting Bright and Cobden, and who later were to supply strength to the Gladstonian Liberal party. They represented the theological elements which went to the making of that party's creed. They also produced a movement within Methodism which was bringing over a section of that hitherto Tory Church into the ranks of British Liberalism.

They attacked what they characterised as the "un-English" nature of their treatment by Conference. They professed to be the champions of free speech, both in Conference and out of it, the guardians of English liberties withheld by those in authority, and the uncompromising enemies of all who would attempt, upon whatever pretext, to tamper with those "rights". Their preference for Liberty, as the greatest of the three French Revolutionary values, was in line with their English Liberalism. Their cult of Freedom and their hostility to Conference rule marched *pari passu* with their *laissez-faire* attack upon

[1] Arthur's sketch of Bunting in *The Christian Times*, 1849. Quoted *Life of Bunting*, II, 348.

governmental action in national affairs. They were, in their public apologetics, avowed individualists, and their individualism inspired both their ecclesiastical and political activities.[1] In spite of the Toryism of Methodist traditions, they were brought over into the Liberal party.

Once the controversy passed from Conference to the public platform the movement began to excite more than a denominational interest. Other Churches expressed their opinions, and national newspapers gave unwonted space to the affairs of a divided Methodism. Especially in the Lancashire and Yorkshire towns, the agitation was accompanied by great excitement and occasional violence,[2] and the public could not help knowing that all was not well with Methodism. Political animosities increased the bitterness of feeling, and, in some parts of the country, that factor for long retarded the progress of the modern Methodist Union movement.

With the exception of *The Christian Times*, the whole of the Nonconformist press supported the "Reformers", and, in no uncertain terms, condemned the policy of "Conference Methodism". Editorial articles were written supporting the stand of the expelled ministers against Conference tyranny, and ranking them with the great champions of that ecclesiastical liberty which it had been the glory of Nonconformity to win; advertisements and reports of their meetings appeared in prominent places

[1] *The Wesleyan Times* for 1849–50 (the period of the great meetings) supplies abundant evidence as to the character of the speeches and arguments of the agitators. See *passim*.

[2] There are many local stories of "incidents" in these stormy days. At Yeadon Everett was shot at. *Life*, p. 436.

in their pages; whilst articles by Everett, Dunn, and Griffith were printed to give Nonconformist readers at first hand a statement of the case against Bunting and his policy. Wesleyan Methodism, by its attitude of splendid isolation, and by its avowed preference for the Church of England, had not made itself popular with Nonconformists, and so, when the opportunity of hitting back presented itself, as it now did, the Dissenting press seized it. Criticism of the paternalism of Wesleyan Methodist Church government had hitherto been stultified by the numerical success of the movement and the zeal of its converts; now it seemed as though the efficient machine was breaking down. Everett and his coadjutors were hailed as saviours of Methodism from the strangling grip of clerical bureaucracy, and as prophets leading their brethren into the promised land of Free Churchmanship. At last, they hoped, Wesleyan Methodism might join the "Minor Methodist" Churches in the ecclesiastical "Left Wing".

Not only was the Nonconformist press ranged on the side of the Reformers, but pulpits were thrown open to them. Baptists, Congregationalists, Primitive, New Connexion, and Association Methodists preached in their favour, and invited them to preach to their congregations. The various minor Methodist bodies welcomed the expelled ministers as fellow-exiles, but it was Congregationalism that exerted the greatest influence on the movement, and that determined the shape it was to take. Everett had been much impressed by the meeting of the Congregational Union at York in 1847,[1] and Griffith was

[1] *Life*, p. 355.

more of an Independent than a Methodist.[1] The movement of which they were the leaders consequently produced a Methodism strongly marked by Congregationalist features. When the project of reform from within had to be abandoned and a new Church organised, the effects of this friendship were clearly seen. The "United Methodist Free Churches" were "Congregational Methodist Churches"[2] and they were unmistakably Nonconformist.

National newspapers also gave space to the progress of the movement. *The Leeds Mercury* had supported the "Nonconformist Methodists" of 1827, and now, as befitted a wider movement, it was the national organ of Liberalism which took up the case. *The Times*, in a leading article, denounced the action of Conference in expelling the three ministers. It took up the case as one involving the freedom of the press, and as concerning the liberties of free-born Englishmen. It attacked Conference as an autocratic body which, in pursuit of its own aggrandisement, was prepared to trample upon the rights of its members and dependents. It blessed the efforts made by the victims of an irresponsible tyranny to reform the constitution of a Church whose political Conservatism it heartily disliked. It saw in their efforts something of the same spirit which had inspired its own worship of "the sacred name of Liberty".

Such assistance was greatly appreciated by reformers

[1] He settled down in Derby at his "Reformed" Chapel in 1858, and gave up the itinerancy.
[2] Their subsequent history, in one aspect, is a story of the conquest of the Congregationalist by the Methodist elements. Methodist Union in 1932 marks for them the completion of that conquest, so far as the connexional life of the Church is concerned.

186

who had named their own newspaper after *The Times*; and they hoped that the national notice which they had attracted would prove useful in the attainment of their ecclesiastical objects. The assistance of the Nonconformist press helped them to recruit Nonconformist sympathies; the publicity given to them by the national press gave them a vehicle by which they might carry into the very market-place their appeal against the injustice of Conference. An appeal, which was to be made to men both inside the Church and outside, was greatly strengthened by the friendly attitude of such a large section of the press. By both types of newspapers was their agitation hailed as a blow for the natural rights of Englishmen, and, on every side, were to be found sympathisers and supporters. A common Liberalism drew them all together to assist an avowedly Liberal movement.

The expulsions and agitations of the years following 1849 were greater in their extent than either party had anticipated. Many of the clerical Liberals drew back from the violence of the controversy, and kept their places in the old Church; but their counsels of moderation were unheeded by their more autocratic brethren. The attacks of the malcontents had stung Conference into extreme actions. In 1850 Beaumont was censured from the chair of Conference for his mild administration of the Sixth London Circuit,[1] and the Circuit memorials which had poured in were unceremoniously thrown out. The "Mediationists", a body of influential and moderate laymen, anxious for reform without violence, could not obtain a hearing when they sought to modify the down-

[1] *Sidelights*, p. 475.

right policy of the majority in Conference. A policy of rigid discipline, without regard to constitutional procedure, was adopted and pressed to its logical conclusion. The year 1851 saw a decrease in membership of over 56,000. Domestic disputes almost paralysed evangelistic activity, and expulsions and secessions were on a large scale. There was not another increase in any year's returns until 1856, and, by that time, 100,000 members had been lost by the Wesleyan Methodist Church.

The size of the movement embarrassed Everett, Dunn, and Griffith. They had claimed that their case represented the view-point of the majority within Methodism, but they had not been prepared for what actually took place. A movement intended to effect internal reforms had become, by reason of the policy of the "Die-Hards", a movement composed of expelled members. Men who had been merely destructive critics of "Methodism as it is"[1] were at a loss to know what should be their policy. They had not worked out any constructive programme of reform, and their decision to lay siege to Conference, as a means of securing eventual reforms, revealed the inadequacy of their policy. When the loss of 100,000 members did not produce any weakening of the resolution of Conference, it became obvious that the Reformers would need to adopt a more positive line of action to secure their success.

Their slowness in realising this, and their reluctance to act as anything but critics of the "Pontificate", gave to their movement a negative aspect not easily dispelled. They had asked men brought up in the traditions of

[1] This was the title of one of Everett's books.

Methodist fellowship to forgo that, in order to win their ecclesiastical rights. They had called upon them to hold out so long as Conference refused to admit their claims, and, in short, to sacrifice their religious needs to the accomplishment of their ecclesiastical desires. The policy of their cry "No Surrender! No Secession! No Supplies!" put too much strain upon the allegiance and endurance of people at heart more interested in spiritual than in ecclesiastical questions. Many fell away from their side, and others returned to the "Old Body", before the expelled ministers decided to form a new Connexion. Others, who had sympathised with the politics of the movement, but whose Methodism had not been sown in deep soil, ceased to be members of either Church. Deserted by Methodists who disliked the Congregationalism of these Liberal leaders, deserted by many who could not permanently sever themselves from their Church, deserted by those who severed all connexion with institutional Christianity, deserted by Dunn himself, Everett and Griffith carried with them into the United Methodist Free Churches only 40,000 members.

They had hesitated too long before taking the decisive step of establishing a Church which should be independent of the Wesleyan Methodist Conference, and their hesitation not only cost them members and support, but robbed their Church of something of the prestige attaching to any embodiment of great and positive ecclesiastical principles. The "New Body" could too easily be characterised by its opponents as the last resort of discontented Methodists, whereas it ought to have stood forth clearly as the greatest expression of Liberal Methodism. Its architects had been lacking in constructive ability; it was as though a demolition gang had been entrusted with the planning and building of a new Church.

The new Church involved considerable modifications of the system of the "Wesleyan Reaction". The elements of Congregationalism which had attracted its leaders found expression in its constitution, and inspired the criticism through which even the most characteristically Methodist features of Connexionalism had to pass. Both Everett and Griffith had found the itinerancy irksome, and accordingly, in the "Free Churches", the rigid "Three Year System"[1] was abandoned and the rules of the itinerancy were made more elastic. Griffith settled down in a newly built "Reformed" chapel in Derby, and several of his colleagues stayed in one Circuit much longer than was customary in Methodism. It is a mark of Congregationalist influence that a movement which began as an attack on "Location" in high places[2] should have issued in a greater measure of localisation amongst Circuit ministers. The itinerant plan was not forsaken— the new Church could hardly have retained the name of Methodist had that happened—but it was made possible, subject to Conferencial sanction, for Circuits to retain their ministers as long as they desired. The new system combined Methodist "Stationing" and the Congregationalist "Call".

The authority of the joint pastorate, acting through Conference, had been one of the strongest forces in

---

[1] By which ministers moved to a fresh Circuit every three years at least.

[2] See the *Fly Sheets*.

Wesleyan Methodism. Its "Connexional Committees" had formed that "overmighty Executive" against which the Reformers had flung themselves, and by the decision of which they had been expelled. The "Free Churches", in their Constitution, not only tried to guard against a recurrence of tyranny by the executive, but curbed the power of the joint pastorate itself. They were determined that ministers in the United Methodist Free Churches should never be able to think of themselves as members of an exclusive and irresponsible caste. They felt that it was only because the Wesleyan ministers had been accountable to one another, instead of to their people, that the arrogant injustice of the expulsions had been possible. They did not adopt the Congregationalist system of the responsibility of a minister to his church alone, but by vindicating the principle of "Circuit Independence" under the sovereignty of Conference, they combined elements of both traditions. The ministry in the new body had a dual responsibility—to the Circuits and to the popularly elected Conference;[1] the ministry in the old body was, owing to the nature of Conference, irresponsible.

The rallying cry of the Reformers had been "No Sacerdotalism". They carried the spirit of that cry into their church life. "Wesleyan Reform" had been a movement composed for the most part of disgruntled laymen, and its constitution and ἦθος alike bore the marks of its genesis. On its positive side, the cardinal principle of

[1] Representation of the Circuits at Conference was determined by the vote of the Circuit Quarterly Meeting, and either laymen or ministers might be elected. This was Eckett's unshakeable principle. *Vide supra*, p. 158.

"Free Methodism" may be described as a practical belief in the Protestant doctrine of the "Priesthood of All Believers"; on its negative side, it was a thoroughgoing Anti-Clericalism. It was this attitude which was responsible for most of the modifications of the Wesleyan Reaction embodied in the constitution of the Free Churches. As it had inspired resistance to the rule of Conference, so now it played its part in restraining clericalism in the new Methodism which the events of 1849–51 had produced.

The malcontents of this period would have read Daniel Isaac's *Examination of Clerical Claims*[1] with enthusiasm, and they would have found, in those pages so obnoxious to the Wesleyan Methodist Conference, arguments to vindicate their own position. Their treatment at the hands of autocratic Superintendents, who had arbitrarily withheld their class tickets, taken away their class books and plans, and denied them appeal against their sentences, had embittered many Methodist laymen. They determined to tolerate no such treatment in their own Connexion, and, not only did they constitutionally limit the power of their pastors, but they watched them with suspicion, lest they should make any attempts to exalt their office. No hierarchy could flourish in so hostile an atmosphere. Griffith, who was acclaimed as the "Luther of the Movement",[2] and who was its most forcible apologist, would neither wear clerical costume nor assume the title "Reverend". He was an avowed Nonconformist and used to sign his letters "William Griffith— New Testament Bishop". His attitude was character-

[1] *Vide supra*, pp. 161–2.　　[2] See *The Wesleyan Times, passim.*

istic of that of his supporters: a denial of privilege and an assertion of "rights".

It had been assumed in the "Reaction" that, by virtue of their divine call to the ministry, Methodist preachers had been given authority over their flocks, and that, in the discharge of this trust from God, they were responsible only to Him and to Conference. Bunting had even stated that, in certain matters, the Voice of Conference might be held to be equivalent to the Voice of God.[1] This doctrine the Reformers totally rejected. They regarded their ministers as servants of their congregations rather than the congregations as subjects of their preachers. The prayer: "O Lord, bless the work of our servant, Thy minister!"[2] was typical of their attitude towards the pastoral office. Wesleyan controversialists had minimised the part played by laymen in the Church; the apologists of a Church, which, especially in its early years, had to place great reliance on the efforts of its laymen, went to the opposite extreme, and denied any special virtue in the Pastorate. If the Wesleyans, in their reverence for the ministerial status, had developed certain Catholic elements of John Wesley's "Reaction in the Evolution of Protestantism", the Free Methodists swung over to a purely Protestant position.

Hopes were entertained that the disruption of 1849–56 might result in the formation of one Liberal Methodist Connexion which should unite all those who had at any time protested against "Conference Methodism". The negotiations, however, came to nothing, owing to the insistence by the United Methodist Free Churches upon

[1] *Vide supra*, p. 128 n. 1. [2] Quoted *N.H.M.* I, 538.

Circuit independence, and upon the right of Circuits to nominate their representatives to Conference from either ministers or laymen, and not according to the Methodist New Connexion's scheme of alternating representation. Upon this rock the proposals for union in 1835 had foundered, and such union was not to be achieved for another half century.[1]

The dogma of Circuit independence was not only an obstacle to Liberal Methodist union, but also an example of how the "Liberals" rejected the principles of the "Reaction". The name "United Methodist Free Churches" not only implied the union of two Churches on an equal footing, but also indicated the strength of the Congregationalist element in that Connexion. In the last of the Methodist Churches formed by a revolt of the spirit of Liberalism against the power of authority, Connexionalism had to fight hard to keep its place against the claims of "Circuit Independence". The prejudices of Free Methodists caused them to distrust the Connexional system as being liable to encourage clerical solidity, and that "excrescence of Popery—the doctrine of the divine right of absolute rule over the Church".

The movement from which "Free Methodism" was born was a laymen's movement, and the influence of Independent traditions upon its constitution derived its greatest force from this fact. Not only did these expelled laymen come into daily contact with Congregationalists

---

[1] By the formation, in 1907, of the United Methodist Church, which brought together the United Methodist Free Churches, the Methodist New Connexion, and the Bible Christians.

of their own class, but they found in the ecclesiastical thinking of the Independents many points of contact with their own Liberalism. The attraction of Congregationalism lay in its tradition of liberty—that liberty which was regarded by the Liberal Methodist laymen as the supreme ecclesiastical and political value.

CHAPTER VIII

METHODISM IN 1851: ITS
POLITICAL TYPES

The developments of sixty years had transformed Methodism. Under the guidance of John Wesley it had been militarily organised to fulfil its work of evangelism, and from him it had received its peculiar character. In its growth from a set of "United Societies" into a powerful Denomination it had been led to discard some parts of "Mr Wesley's Plan" and to modify others, to strengthen some and to weaken others, and unconsciously to revolutionise the whole. The emergence of new types, and especially the Liberal, had hastened the changes, and had led to the devastating schisms of those sixty years. Under Wesley, at the beginning of the period, Methodism was united in the bond of one spirit and one allegiance; under Bunting, at the end of it, Wesleyan Methodism, torn by faction, seething with discontent, and bewildered by agitation, was but the largest of several Methodist Connexions. Both in spirit and in organisation, the Methodism of 1851 contrasted with that of 1791.

Until 1791 Methodist history had had a unity it has never known since, the unity which John Wesley's supremacy had given to it; from 1791 to 1851 it was the story of divisions and clashes between rival systems and conflicting principles. The ecclesiastical turmoil and evangelistic paralysis of 1851 contrasted sharply with the peaceful fellowship and aggressive evangelism of the Methodism of Wesley's later days. At both times there was a strong man governing the Church, but Bunting was not the "Father of his People" in the way that Wesley had been. Love and respect for Wesley had kept the discontented elements quiet in 1791; hatred and jealousy of the "Pope of Methodism" had supplied the occasions for those schisms which scattered Methodists into hostile camps in 1851. The authority of Wesley had been borne willingly by people who were devoted to him; that of Bunting could not be imposed upon people who felt they had outgrown the need for leading strings. The unity Methodism lost with the death of Wesley was not to be regained till 1932.[1] The tempestuous year 1851 may be taken as the date when the spirit of schism was most active in Methodism. It was in that year that Wesleyan Methodism reported a decrease of 56,068 members.

But not only did Methodism lose its unity in this period; it moved away from its "Reactionary" position, and became simply the greatest but most hierarchical of the Nonconformist Churches in England; it wasted Wesley's sacramental legacy; it forsook his belief in the Church as the Body of Christ, and substituted for his High Churchmanship an ideal of Pastoral Supremacy. Where he had been Catholic, it became authoritarian. There is a fundamental difference between the spirit of Wesley's *Apology* in 1766[2] and that of Bunting's defence

[1] Even now the reunion has not been complete. The Independent Methodists (10,796 members) and the Wesleyan Reform Union (13,828 members) still remain outside the united Church. The Independent Methodists have no separated ministry. [Figures 1931.]   [2] *Supra*, pp. 45–7.

of Conference.[1] With Bunting the "Wesleyan Reaction" had become so materialised that it could not survive. The stereotyped method of evangelism and the individualistic type of churchmanship[2] which marked the new Methodism were both manifestations of the spirit which brought about the break-up of the Reaction.

What was true of Wesleyan Methodism was equally true of the other Methodist Churches which made up the opposition to Wesleyanism. To the modifications adopted by the "Old Body" they added "the dissidence of Dissent". For the sake of their ecclesiastical ideals they had been ready to leave the Church of their fathers, and to set up in opposition Connexions which would embody their principles. Wesleyan Methodism had drifted away from Anglicanism, and the Wesleyans always kept a sentimental regard for their Mother Church; the "Free" Methodists had either been expelled or had deliberately seceded from the Wesleyan Church, and they did not sentimentalise over the old attachment. "Conference Methodism" they regarded as a type of popery which must be fought at all costs. They set no store by the truly Catholic elements in John Wesley's theology and practice, and they regarded as infringements of the natural rights of man all clerical claims or privileges. They justly regarded themselves as Nonconformists, and they had no hesitation in attacking the privileges of the Anglican Church.

John Wesley would scarcely have recognised the Methodism of sixty years after his death. Divided by different organisations, disturbed by violent agitators,

[1] *Supra*, pp. 127–9.   [2] *Vide supra*, pp. 101–3.

devoting time to ecclesiastical instead of to spiritual considerations, using the piety of his brother Charles in a mechanical way, failing, in consequence, to write hymns such as were written by the first generation of Methodists,[1] preaching "revivalist" sermons of a set type, making much of Hell Fire in its appeal to the individual conscience,[2] standardising the experience of conversion, making little of the Sacraments and the Church, enthroning "Order" by the side of "Faith", or superseding "Order" by "Rights", a hierarchical Dissent facing a group of Liberal Dissenting Churches, instead of a Protestant expression of the Holy Catholic Church: such was the Methodism of 1851. John Wesley would have regarded it with a curious and, probably, a sad gaze. It bore but little semblance to the Methodism he had directed until his death in 1791.

He would, too, have regarded Methodist politics with surprise. His advice to his followers to abstain from too active an interest in party politics had been interpreted by the Wesleyan Methodist Conference in such a way as to strengthen all the Conservative and Tory elements in the Connexion, and such an interpretation had provoked the Liberalism of the Methodist dissentients into an open expression of hostility to Conference. Down to 1791, even Liberals like Kilham had not felt the prohibition of political activity by the "Father of Methodism" to be any real hardship. They realised that he had given such a ruling to prevent spiritual needs being neglected in the

---

[1] *Vide supra*, pp. 99–100.
[2] Wesley himself rarely preached "Hell Fire Sermons". He much more often "offered Christ" to his congregations. See *Journal, passim.*

interests of political, and they considered the price he demanded not unreasonable. The rigidifying of a paternal rule made a difference, especially when men of Liberal sympathies felt that there was unjust discrimination against them. Paradoxically, the "No Politics Rule" increased party heats in Methodism.

But if John Wesley would have been surprised at this unfortunate development of his own good intentions, it must be remembered that, not only had Methodism changed between 1791 and 1851, but so had conditions in England. More important still, the men who had become Methodists were different. The sixty years of this study cover a period of great acceleration in the progress of the Industrial Revolution. They were also years of important social, constitutional, and political changes, and those changes left their mark on Methodism, and on the political life of Methodists.

The trumpet call of the French Revolution had broken the sleep of the eighteenth century and had sounded in the ears of classes hitherto politically unself-conscious. Liberty, Equality, and Fraternity were universal values, and their proclamation in 1789 gave inspiration to the English middle and working classes in launching that movement which culminated in the Reform Bill of 1832. Methodism might denounce the Revolution, and feed its Conservatism on its horror of revolutionary violence; but it could not prevent the leavening of its members' minds by the new ideas which the events of 1789 had let loose upon the world. Methodism was opposed to the French Revolution in almost all its manifestations; but many individual Methodists were brought under its spell.

What the French Revolution began, the great ideals of nineteenth-century politics, the extension of the franchise, local government reform, Chartism, Disestablishment, and Free Trade, carried forward.[1] Politics were becoming, not a merely aristocratic preserve, but a common interest and a topic of conversation throughout the country. In the new industrial centres, where Methodism was strongest, men shared their ideas and political views. Methodists came to realise what were their political interests, and to demand the vindication of their political rights against the privileges of both Church and aristocracy. Liberty, Equality, and Fraternity were not unlike the values they had come to associate with their religion, and that gave to them an added sanction. The laymen of this period, who became interested in politics through their daily contacts, were often sympathetic towards the political ambitions of their own class, and they could not be dragooned by the decisions of their pastors. Exhortations by Conference to keep clear of politics fell with little effect upon ears accustomed to the daily discussion of political questions in shop and factory. Whichever side they might take, it was becoming more and more plain that the Reform Bill and the Municipal Corporations Act of 1835 had roused the interests and given expression to the hopes of a new political class. The "No Politics Rule" could no longer be enforced upon a laity deeply stirred by political ideals.

In place of the peace and homogeneity of 1791 there was in 1851 a double fissure in Methodism: half ecclesiastical and half political. It was the result of the break-up

[1] See Chapter VI.

of the Reaction, and its two aspects, as results of the same spirit, bore more than a superficial resemblance to each other. It has been noticed how almost all the leaders of movements for ecclesiastical reform in Methodism have in politics been Liberals, and the significance of this fact lies in its relation to the Liberalism of their followers. Not only were the leaders of the reforming movements Liberals, but so were the rank and file of the "Minor Methodist" Churches. The two ecclesiastical camps within Methodism corresponded to the two political camps it contained. The Wesleyans championed authority in Church and State, and were Tories; the Free Methodists raised the standard of liberty, and were avowed Liberals. That was the chief characteristic of the political life of Methodism in 1851, and it is of the greatest importance in estimating the causes for the changes in Methodism's political alliances in the nineteenth century.

The "respectable Wesleyans", upon whom the Tory electioneering agents in Disraeli's *Coningsby* relied, were men of a new political type. The Whigs had been baffled by the politics of this new Dissent,[1] and the Tories had never previously been accustomed to count for support on a body of Dissenters. Yet here were Dissenters, who disliked being classed as such, who had little sympathy with the Dissenting appeal against Disestablishment, who eschewed the alliance with the Whigs, and who denounced "Political Dissenters" as more interested in politics than in religion, who disliked Liberalism and Radicalism for their atheistic associations, who had heartily opposed that "victory of Liberalism over Evan-

[1] Halévy, I, 405.

gelicalism",[1] Roman Catholic Emancipation, who had
disliked the agitation for the Reform Bill, and whose
non-political attitude might be used against the ambitions
of aggressive reformers. Such men, Disraeli believed,
might be recruited for a new Conservative party. Never
before could that have been possible, but never before
had there been such Dissenters in England.

The Wesleyan Methodist Tory—"and possibly the
majority of the Wesleyans were Tories"[2]—was the product of a reaction in the evolution of English Nonconformity. Whilst accepting many of the practical conse-
quences of his Nonconformist position, he remained
friendly in his attitude towards the Church of England.
He attended services at the parish church as well as at
his own chapel, and, whenever possible, he preferred to
communicate there. He valued the tradition of his origin
within the National Church; he, like the Anglican, was
an Arminian, whilst the Dissenter was either a Calvinist
or a Unitarian; he, like the Anglican, if not an Episcopalian, was, in Church government, a supporter of
clerical supremacy and ecclesiastical solidarity, whilst
the Dissenter was a democrat and a particularist; he,
like the Anglican, was a loyalist, whilst many a Dissenter
was a Radical or even a Republican.

The Wesleyan Tory was not so much a Tory by choice
as by the necessity of circumstances. He was the most
vigorous advocate of the "No Politics" principle. In-
heriting all the fear of John Wesley lest political activity

[1] Halévy, II, 276.
[2] Halévy, III, 156. This volume contains quite an accurate
estimate of Wesleyan politics in this period.

should lead to spiritual sterility, he transmuted Wesley's advice into a repressive rule which defeated its own object, and divided Methodism into two political camps. Compelled by the circumstances of his daily life and contacts to take political sides, he applied the negative principles of his political quietism, and resisted the political philosophy of those who were working for social and constitutional change. Where his companions were inspired by Liberal and Radical ideals, he reacted against them and supported the existing *régime*. In effect he became a Tory. He might parade his hostility to "Political Dissenters" and his own isolation from political factions, but his support of "Church and King", and his hatred of Radicals, led him further and further into a tacit association with Conservative forces in the national life.

There was, too, a positive side to this political attitude. Not only did the Wesleyan Tory dislike the principles and practice of Liberals, but he found elements in his own creed which he could not reconcile with the political ideals of those whom he disliked as the perverters of his associates. He saw Liberalism, not only as the political creed of atheists and unspiritual Dissenters,[1] but also as the inspiration for those malcontents who had torn his own Church with their divisive ideas. If Liberalism stood for all he hated, both in Church and State, Toryism contained the same elements of respect for authority

---

[1] To characterise all Nonconformist politicians as "unspiritual Dissenters" was patently unfair, especially in view of the personnel of the English Nonconformist Denominations, but there were enough men of this type amongst the "Old Denominations" to lend colour to this generalisation of the "Wesleyan Tory".

that characterised Methodism. If Liberalism disturbed the peace of Methodism, Toryism was a political expression of what the nineteenth-century Wesleyan Tory came to look upon as the guiding principle of his Church, the principle to defend which he was prepared to cast out all who disagreed with it. Bunting's "Methodism hates democracy as much as it hates sin" was a positive as well as a negative statement.

The Wesleyan Tory, who, in 1851, whole-heartedly supported the autocratic policy of the Conference party, had drawn his inspiration from a variety of sources. His application of the "No Politics Rule", which had impelled him to resist the activity of reformers, his respect for the Church of England and his dislike of the negative character of the agitation for Disestablishment, his fear and hatred of the *fons et origo* of Liberalism—the French Revolution, his loyalty to the Crown, the undemocratic nature of his own Church government, and the positive authoritarianism to which he gave his support—all these were factors moulding the attitude of the Wesleyan Tory. His influence, both in Methodism and in national affairs, was great. To him in particular did the nation owe whatever political contributions Methodism had made towards saving England from a Revolution akin to that in France.

The Methodist Liberal, whose development has been traced throughout this period, was a more complex character than his Tory counterpart. The Tories were almost all Wesleyan Methodists, but, if the Free Methodist Churches were predominantly Liberal, there was a Liberal section in the Church they had all left at one time or another. The Methodist Liberal's attitude to ecclesiastical and political matters comprised elements drawn from various sources, and it found expression in different ways. His outlook had not the homogeneity of that of the Methodist Tory, but his influence in changing the character of Methodism, and in building the Gladstonian Liberal Party, was commensurate with the Conservative influence of his rival.

Griffith, one of the leaders of the agitation which was tearing Wesleyan Methodism in 1851,[1] was, of all the Free Methodists' leaders, the most open and virulent Liberal. He had been an electioneering agent for M. T. Bass in Derby, and had been more advanced than his patron. He was unashamed of his Liberalism and, although he was more extreme than many of his supporters, he was convinced that his political views were only an expression of his belief. "If I am a Chartist, my Bible has made me so."[2]

He held that he could not separate religion and politics, and that a "No Politics Rule" to protect the interests of religion was a contradiction in terms. This was one of the elements in Griffith's position which gave to his enemies a mark for their shafts. In a Church convinced of the danger of politics in the pulpit, Griffith refused to bow to the ruling of Conference and the sentiment of the Connexion. He had caused trouble by this attitude before 1849, and, after his expulsion, he continued to preach political sermons, and to carry on the active

[1] His followers called him "The Luther of the Reform Movement". See advertisements in *The Wesleyan Times* for 1849 onwards.
[2] Reported in *Life*, p. 179.

local and national political work in which he had been engaged.[1]

In refusing to separate religion and politics, or to keep politics out of Methodist pulpits—and in this Griffith was by no means alone—the Methodist Liberal gave to his political opinions a theological colouring. Inspired by his doctrines of Salvation and Assurance, he questioned all forms of ecclesiastical or political privilege. If men are equal in the sight of God, then, argued Griffith, they ought to share equally the privileges of social, religious, and political life. Universal Franchise, Disestablishment, and Anti-Clericalism were, for the Methodist Liberal, all linked with his interpretation of this doctrine of Assurance, an interpretation which was a common constituent of Methodist Liberalism throughout the period from Kilham to Griffith.

The rejection of the "No Politics Rule" led to political activity, especially in the industrial north and midlands. Here the Methodist Liberal took his place in the movement for gaining political rights for the middle and working classes of the new towns; and, as he himself usually belonged to those classes, he was active in making use of such rights, once they were obtained. As the party of Parliamentary Reform, as the party which, after 1832, took upon itself the championship of the classes it had enfranchised, and as the party to which most of the still

[1] Chew, in Chapter IX of his *Life and Letters of William Griffith*, deals with the politics of this ardent Methodist Liberal. He throws considerable light upon the political ideals of this type of man, but, in Griffith, this idealism took a somewhat exaggerated form. The average Liberal Methodist was usually less extreme than his ministerial leader of 1849–57.

unenfranchised working classes looked for the reward for their patience and support, the Whig-Liberal party reaped the benefit of this activity. It was no mere accident that the Methodist Liberal was usually an inhabitant of one of the large industrial centres. It was there that both ecclesiastical and political Liberalism affected Methodism most.

Controversies, such as those concerning Free Trade or Protection, which were agitating the country in 1851, and which had reached fever heat in 1846, when the Corn Laws were repealed, had added to the forces at work in shaping the political character of the Methodist Liberal. Manufacturers and artisans alike desired cheap food, and they cast their influence on the side of those who were working in Parliament for that object. By 1851, in fact, economic considerations had come in to reinforce the old religious and political motives which had outlined the English parties. Free Trade economics appealed to the Methodist Liberal because their practical application was likely to increase his prosperity, and this factor of self-interest had a special attraction for manufacturers and traders such as many of the Methodist Liberals were.

The appeal of Free Trade was not purely economic. In it the Liberal saw a movement, not simply towards economic prosperity and increased profits, but towards the extension of the sphere of individual initiative at the expense of State control. It was this which put it into line with true Liberal thought, and which, quite apart from its economic implications, made the Methodist Liberal desire it. He had come to his political opinions, not simply through the ordinary channels which led into other contemporary Liberalism, but through the ecclesiastical controversies which had disturbed his religious life. In consequence, he was particularly open to the individualist reasoning of the opponents of the State. He saw political Liberalism as the force which was struggling against privilege and authority in the State as he had struggled against it in Methodism, and he thought of his political and ecclesiastical Liberalism as two aspects of the same principle.

His religion had done much to strengthen the self-reliance of the Methodist Liberal. Not only had his creed, like that of the Quakers, tended to produce men well qualified to rise by their own efforts into the position of "Captains of Industry", but the Puritanism of Methodism had restricted the amusements open to its members. Forbidden many of the amusements which might have lightened the oppressive seriousness of his life, the Methodist Liberal had turned his concentrated attention upon business and upon political and ecclesiastical questions. The crowded conditions of life in urban districts encouraged a repressive tendency, of which the Sabbatarianism of Methodism was one manifestation. The result was the growth of that "well off" middle class portrayed in Mark Rutherford's novels. Its sturdy independence made its members well disposed towards the *laissez-faire* policy of Liberalism. To men who had risen by their own character and efforts, the idea that the State should interfere with their trade or the running of their businesses seemed but to encourage unwarranted and inefficient meddling.

The various seeds from which the Methodist Liberal

had sprung had come to fruition by 1851. The violent controversies of that year bore testimony to his existence, and the nature of his arguments to the authenticity of his Liberalism. It became evident in 1851 that the predominant Toryism of Wesleyan Methodism was by no means the universal political faith of Methodists. Previous disruptions had been regarded as isolated cases of discontent with the personal influence of certain powerful individuals; by 1851 it was possible to see that they were ebullitions of a Liberal spirit which all the power of the Conservative majority could not succeed in silencing. The events of 1851 revealed the unexpected strength of Liberal Methodism. The common characteristics of the movements of 1797, 1827, 1835, and 1849–57 demonstrated their essential unity as manifestations of that spirit of protest, in the name of liberty, against irresponsible authority, which, throughout this study, has been regarded as the fundamental characteristic of Liberalism.

So produced, the Methodist Liberal presented a definite contrast to the Methodist Tory. The Tory was a Royalist; the Liberal, when not a Republican (as Griffith avowedly was), was at any rate opposed to the exercise of the Prerogative, and was prepared to support the "Constitution" against all interference by the Crown. The Tory regarded the House of Lords as an essential and valuable part of the English Constitution;[1] the Liberal echoed the young Disraeli's remark that the real use of the Upper House was to record the decisions of the Lower.

[1] See *The Watchman's* political news, and contrast that in *The Wesleyan Times*.

The Tory respected the aristocracy; the Liberal took every opportunity of expressing his contempt for men whom only the accident of birth had raised above men worthier in most cases than they were. The Tory, as he believed in the enlightened rule of the ministry in ecclesiastical matters, favoured aristocratic government in the State; the Liberal, denouncing "Conference Methodism" as an excrescence of popery, carried his democratic ideals into the sphere of politics, and demanded an equal share for all men in the business of electing representatives in Parliament. The Tory was a Protectionist and disliked Cobden; the Liberal was a Free Trader who regarded Cobden as one of his heroes. The Tory was proud of the Army and Navy; the Liberal resented the uneconomic expense of the Services.[1] The Tory disliked the Nonconformists and supported the Establishment; the Liberal held that, for members of a "Parliamentary Church" to talk of "Political Dissenters" was a case of the beam and the mote.[2]

If it be added that, with these differences of outlook, there was a social and occupational difference between many representatives of both types, the contrast will be seen to be clearer than ever. This cleavage was not so distinct as that involved by their rival ideas, but it had a share in intensifying the differences. In the Wesleyan Methodist ministry the Tories greatly outnumbered the Liberals, and, with the exception of individuals, the ministry may be taken as being solidly Tory. Methodist

[1] *The Wesleyan Times* did not follow *The Daily News* in its support of Palmerston's swashbuckling foreign policy. Its heroes were Bright and Cobden, who were consistently peace-loving.

[2] See *Life and Letters of William Griffith*, p. 159.

Liberalism was a layman's movement. In the country districts there were few Liberal Methodists, and the ordinary Wesleyan farmer or country tradesman was a Tory. Fear that the repeal of the Corn Laws would ruin them naturally made them Tories.

It was in the industrial towns that the clashes occurred. There were to be found Tories amongst tradesmen and manufacturers, and especially amongst wealthy and respectable laymen, whose rise in the social scale had brought with it a settled Conservatism which made them tender towards the aristocracy whose ranks they might hope one day to enter. Snobbery played its part in making Tories. There was always a social gulf between Churchman and Dissenter, and there were many bourgeois Methodists who kept up their connexion with the parish church because of these social distinctions. On the other hand, many of these middle-class Methodists loved and respected their ministers and disliked the attacks made upon them by the Liberals. They supported a system of clerical government of the Church because they believed it to be both efficient and scriptural. If some of the Tories were snobbish, others were indubitably sincere in the profession of their ecclesiastico-political faith.

It was, however, from this class, and especially from the lower-middle class, that Methodist Liberals were drawn. They were almost confined to it at this period, and they formed the strength of the United Methodist Free Churches, which were formed into a Connexion in 1857. Most of them were men who had risen by their own efforts, and who were consequently filled with a sense of their own worth and importance. They could not bear to see factitious aristocracies, or to be ruled by despots, however benevolent. They rejected the idea of government not by but for the people, which had been the main idea of Conference rule, and they demanded, as their right, a share in the direction of their affairs. Theirs, in full measure, was that "Dissidence of Dissent" which, by leading them to attack privilege and paternalism, gave them their place in the battle for ecclesiastical and political liberty which English Nonconformity has waged from the sixteenth century onwards. If there were Methodist Liberals whose attitude was determined by motives of self-interest, and of the negative dislike of their more influential neighbours, there were others who realised something of the splendour of the cause for which they were fighting in 1851, both in their Church and in the State.

In this study of Methodist politics down to 1851 the names "Liberal" and "Tory" have been used generally, rather than "Whig" and "Conservative", with a view to their meaning, rather than to their historic conjunctions. The word "Liberal" implies that belief in liberty which has been taken as the chief element in the creed of the Methodist type under consideration, and it may be said to involve "Whiggism" as one of its parts. "Tory", better than "Conservative", suggests the guiding principle of authoritarianism, and it has been used as a more comprehensive term in relation to the beliefs held by Methodists of this type. "Tory" includes "Conservative" in the same way as "Liberal" "Whig". (Possibly the modern usage of "Tory" bears witness to this?) If it be objected that these more comprehensive terms do not find support in historical juxtaposition, it may be said that the study of Methodism and Politics down to 1851 is a study of political types and alignments rather than of definite political alliances, and, as such, it has been thought justifiable to use these more general terms in order to emphasise the fundamental, as against the circumstantial, difference between them.

Such a study has its place in the story of the Dissenting-Liberal alliance. It points to some of the most important factors which have cemented it and held it together for three centuries, and it helps in the understanding of both the nature and permanence of that alliance which has given to English Liberalism a character quite unlike that of any continental Liberalism. It is this which gives the study its true historical importance.

The Methodism of 1791 was, doctrinally, ecclesiastically, and politically, a "Reaction in the Evolution of Protestantism". Its Catholic piety, its Sacramental High Churchmanship, its Arminian theology; its centralised organisation, its hierarchical government, its stress upon the fellowship of the class meeting; its political quietism or its championship of authority in the State: all these were elements not usually to be found in English Protestantism.[1] The essential Individualism of Protestantism it had modified by its doctrine of the Church, and Wesley had rejected the "solitary religion" of many Protestants, quite as definitely as he eschewed Roman Catholic Ultramontanism.[2] Neither an entire

[1] By Protestantism here is meant especially Nonconformity. Anglicanism was not so much a "Reaction", as a compromise between Catholicism and Protestantism.

[2] *Vide supra*, p. 47.

214

"Protestant" nor a Papist, he occupies a unique position in the history of the Church.

In the sixty years between 1791 and 1851 the "Wesleyan Reaction" ceased to exist as an active force. Methodism joined the other Protestant Churches, and, in so doing, it took over the ecclesiastical and political traditions of English Nonconformity. Wesleyan Methodism, on the right wing of Nonconformity, had moved least in the Protestant direction. It still retained stronger clerical elements than did the other Methodist bodies, and its political affinities were still more Tory than were those of the others. The "Liberal Methodists" (to give them their own chosen name) had become completely Protestant Churches, and, like the other Nonconformists, had become Liberals in politics.

That common Liberalism was the fruit of similar seeds. Nonconformity made its strongest appeal to the middle classes and the educated artisans—its intellectual appeal, through its great medium of preaching, and the plainness of its ritual, gave it a different constituency from that of Anglicanism—and such were the men who formed the backbone of the Liberal party. The social stigma attached to Nonconformity demanded of its adherents a strength of character which reinforced the "Dissidence of Dissent" which it called forth. Such an element of protest against the generally accepted standard is a peculiarly Liberal trait. In these matters the Liberal Methodist of 1851 was at one with the other Nonconformists, and, slowly but surely, Wesleyan Methodism itself was moving in that direction.

Important as these elements of Dissenting Liberalism

are—and they have largely determined the temper of Liberals of this type—they are not its fundamental principles. Those fundamental principles, as revealed by the history of Methodism's simultaneous gravitation towards Dissent and Liberalism, are two in number, but one in essence: Individualism and Liberty.

It is not too much to say that Nonconformity has been the English Antigone.[1] Liberalism has been the political creed of the individualist striving to be free from the control of the State; Nonconformity has been the religion of the man who could not rest content with the Church of the nation. The Anglican ideal of the Church has been that of the nation on its religious side; the Nonconformist ideal that of a fellowship of the elect, called out of the world. Nonconformity has historically been allied with the Whig-Liberal party, and has found with it a community of interest; but that alliance has been based upon factors greater than historical exigencies. It has been based upon the same spirit: the spirit of liberty protesting against the iron hand of authority. That spirit in England has been, because of English Dissent, a religious spirit, inspired and fed by the Bible, which the Dissenters took as their only charter. The struggle for religious liberty came first; that for political liberty followed it, and in both did the Dissenters take the lead.

[1] Ernest Barker, *Church, State, and Study*, p. 154.

SELECT BIBLIOGRAPHY

This bibliography is not intended to comprehend the whole field surveyed in the essay, but to show which books have been found valuable. For wider reading a student may be recommended to consult the bibliographies appended to either Piette, *John Wesley, Sa Réaction dans l'Évolution du Protestantisme*, or Edwards, *John Wesley and the Eighteenth Century*. Some of the books mentioned, like that of Edwards, have been published since this essay was submitted for the Thirlwall Prize, but they have been useful in revision. The abbreviations used in footnotes are expressed in parenthesis.

The bibliography is arranged alphabetically, but certain books bearing most directly upon the subject are marked *.

BACKGROUND OF THE PERIOD

BARKER, ERNEST. *Church, State, and Study.*
—— *Political Thought in England from Herbert Spencer to to-day.*
DAVIDSON, W. L. *Political Thought in England: The Utilitarians from Bentham to J. S. Mill.*
DICEY, A. V. *Law and Public Opinion in England in the Nineteenth Century* (Dicey).
FAY, C. R. *Great Britain from Adam Smith to the present day.*
*HALÉVY, ÉLIE. *History of the English People in* 1815 (Halévy, I).

HALÉVY, ÉLIE. *History of the English People* (1815–30) (Halévy, II).

—— *History of the English People* (1830–41) (Halévy, III).

LECKY, W. E. H. *History of England in the Eighteenth Century*.

SOMERVELL, D. C. *English Thought in the Nineteenth Century*.

TREVELYAN, G. M. *History of England*.

—— *England under Queen Anne*.

RELIGION AND SOCIAL CONDITIONS, ETC.

ALLEN, G. W. *Methodism and Modern World Problems*.

BREADY, WESLEY. *Lord Shaftesbury*.

BUTTERWORTH, J. *History of Oldham* (1817).

CARTER, HENRY. *The Social Dynamic and the Methodist Movement*.

CECIL, LORD HUGH. *Conservatism*.

CHAMBERS, J. D. *Nottinghamshire in the Eighteenth Century*.

*EDWARDS, MALDWYN. *John Wesley and the Eighteenth Century* (Edwards).

GARVIN, J. L. *Life of Joseph Chamberlain*.

HAMMOND, J. L. and B. *The Age of the Chartists*.

—— *Lord Shaftesbury*.

—— *The Town Labourer*.

HOBHOUSE, L. T. *Liberalism*.

MANNING, B. L. *Making of Modern English Religion*.

MARTIN, H. (ed.). *Christian Social Reformers of the Nineteenth Century*.

MIDDLETON, J. *Oldham Past and Present*.

PEARSON, HESKETH. *The Smith of Smiths*.

PILKINGTON, W. *Methodism in Preston and the Relation of Methodism to the Temperance and Teetotal Movements*.

BIBLIOGRAPHY

SELBIE, W. B. *Nonconformity*.

TAWNEY, R. H. *Religion and the Rise of Capitalism*.

TELFORD, J. *A Sect that moved the World* (on the Clapham Sect).

TROELTSCH, ERNST. *Social Teaching of the Christian Churches*.

*WARNER, W. J. *The Wesleyan Movement and the Industrial Revolution* (Warner).

WEBB, SIDNEY. *The Story of the Durham Miner*.

METHODIST AUTHORITIES

(a) Primary Authorities

Minutes of Conference of the various Methodist Connexions (Minutes)

Journal of the Rev. John Wesley (Journal).

John Wesley's Letters (8 vols.).

Works of John Wesley (32 vols.) (for his pamphlets, hymn books, etc.) (*Works*).

PEIRCE, WILLIAM. *Ecclesiastical Polity of the Wesleyan Methodists* (Peirce).

(b) Secondary Authorities

Lives of the Methodist Preachers (8 vols.).

Proceedings of the Wesley Historical Society (W.H.S. Proceedings).

Publications of the Wesley Historical Society (W.H.S. Publications).

METHODIST HISTORY AND BIOGRAPHY

Articles on Methodism and Methodists in Cambridge Modern History (C.M.H.). Dictionary of National Biography (D.N.B.), and Encyclopaedia Britannica (E.B.).

BAINES-GRIFFITH, D. *Wesley the Anglican.*

BLACKWELL, JOHN. *Life of Alexander Kilham.*

BUNTING, T. P. *Life of Dr Bunting* (2 vols.).

BURBRIDGE, A. *Wesleyanism* (Catholic Truth Society).

CHEW, RICHARD. *James Everett—a biography.*

—— *Life and Letters of William Griffith.*

CLARK, O. A. *Wesley Memorial Volume.*

DIMOND, S. G. *Psychology of the Methodist Revival.*

DINNICK, J. D. *Samuel Dunn—A Memoir.*

EVERETT, JAMES. *Wesleyan Takings, or Centenary Sketches.*

*GREGORY, BENJAMIN. *Sidelights on the Conflicts of Methodism, 1827–52 (Sidelights).*

HARRISON, S. *Companion to the Minutes of Conference of 1849.*

KIRSOP, JOSEPH. *Historical Sketches of Free Methodism.*

LUNN, ARNOLD. *Life of John Wesley.*

*PIETTE, M. *John Wesley, Sa Réaction dans l'Évolution du Protestantisme* (Piette, or *La Réaction Wesléyenne*).

RATTENBURY, J. E. *Wesley's Legacy to the World.*

RIGG, J. H. *The Churchmanship of John Wesley.*

SIMON, J. S. *John Wesley and the Religious Societies.*

—— *John Wesley and the Methodist Societies.*

—— *John Wesley and the Advance of Methodism.*

—— *John Wesley, the Master Builder.*

SMITH, C. *History of Methodism* (3 vols.).

STEAD, W. T. "St John of England" (*Review of Reviews*, 1891).

TAYLOR, ISAAC. *Wesley and Methodism.*

TELFORD, J. *Life of John Wesley.*

TOWNSHEND, W. J., WORKMAN, H. B., and EAYRS, G. *New History of Methodism* (2 vols.) (*N.H.M.*).

BIBLIOGRAPHY

VULLIAMY, C. E. *Life of John Wesley*.

WISEMAN, F. L. *Charles Wesley*.

WORKMAN, H. B. *The Place of Methodism in the Catholic Church*.

—— *Methodism* (Cambridge Manuals).

NEWSPAPERS, PAMPHLETS, ETC.

Pamphlets in the following libraries have been consulted: University Library, Cambridge, Hobill Collection of Methodist literature at Sheffield, Didsbury College, Victoria Park College, Manchester. Those quoted include

ALLIN, T. *An Exposition of the Principles of Church Government adopted by the Methodist New Connexion*.

Centenary of Wesleyan Methodism (Handbook).

General Election of 1892—The Methodist Candidates.

Jubilee of Methodist New Connexion (Handbook).

KILHAM, ALEXANDER. *An Earnest Address to the Preachers assembled in Conference by their affectionate Brethren in the Gospel, Paul and Silas*.

—— *The Progress of Liberty amongst the people called Methodists*, to which is added *The Outlines of a Constitution*.

—— *The Methodist Monitor* (2 vols.).

Papers on Wesleyan Matters.

The Fly Sheets (F.S.).

The Fly Sheets Vindicated.

The Watchman, especially for 1849–51.

The Wesleyan Times, especially for 1849–51.

Vates.

Wesleyan Methodist Magazine.

Other pamphlets, especially those from the Hobill Collection, are referred to in the text under the heading of the volumes in which the late G. A. K. Hobill bound them. This collection is one of the best collections of Methodist literature at present available for research.

INDEX

INDEX

INDEX

Note. For purposes of convenience Methodist preachers have been given the prefix Rev., although they did not assume it until 1818.

For EU product safety concerns, contact us at Calle de José Abascal, 56–1°, 28003 Madrid, Spain or eugpsr@cambridge.org.

www.ingramcontent.com/pod-product-compliance
Ingram Content Group UK Ltd.
Pitfield, Milton Keynes, MK11 3LW, UK
UKHW012328130625
459647UK00009B/139